ABOUT THE BOOK

Dark Tears, Light Tears – Watershed Survivors of Domestic Violence stirs your soul, creating a heavy heart and enlightening it within the same setting. The book highlights a few brave women representing the many. Domestic violence, defined as "any threatening form of mental, emotional, psychological, or physical force against a spouse, intimate partner, person, or a group that either results or is likely to result in injury, or death within the home."[1] The book offers new concepts and valuable insight into the warning signs and characteristics of a potential abuser and why this problem exists. It symbolizes the struggles associated with survivors, and perhaps victims, of domestic abuse and violence. It focuses on Anna Cutters, a self-made female visionary nonprofit executive who overcame an impoverished upbringing under the worst circumstances. Also discussed in this book are the lives of five other courageous women who experienced abusive relationships and shared those experiences with the author.

Dark Tears, Light Tears create awareness and remind us about the devastating effects of domestic violence. Statistics shared in the book support a historical component about abuse, and glorifying moments of survival restore us, reminding us that *weeping endures for a night, but joy comes in the morning.*[2] Dark *Tears, Light Tears* creates no separation between violence committed by an intimate partner within the home and the oppression of other human beings induced by slavery during the 1800s. *Dark Tears, Light Tears* brings controversial and often hidden subject matter to the forefront, such as events involving politics, religion, Christianity, abuse, poverty, and gun control. This book emphasizes the benefits of positive emotions and the impact of negative emotions. Most importantly, this book explains fundamental reasons for not being afraid or ashamed to share stories of abusive relationships. It introduces new perspectives and explores historical events necessary for shaping our futures in a non-abusive manner within the home.

DARK TEARS

LIGHT TEARS

BRENDA J. LEWIS, PhD

DARK TEARS
LIGHT TEARS

WATERSHED SURVIVORS OF DOMESTIC ABUSE

MILL CITY PRESS

Mill City Press, Inc.
2301 Lucien Way #415
Maitland, FL 32751
407.339.4217
www.millcitypress.net

Paperback ISBN-13: 978-1-6628-2675-7
Ebook ISBN-13: 978-1-6628-2676-4

ACKNOWLEDGMENTS

First, to Anna, for allowing me to tell her story of heartache, pain, and joy. You made me re-live my life experiences with every word, and I am a better person because of it. To my husband, Austin, thank you for helping to make our house a peaceful home. To my three sons, Charles, Algarnon, and Jason, planted within my soul is your lifetime of continued support in everything that I do and have done; thank you. To Grace, Emma, Corona, Allison, and Nicollette: thank you for sharing your stories. Although your names were changed to protect your identities, understandably, it was not easy to share, so, again, I thank you. To my sister Daisy L. Thomas, who will always be my biggest cheerleader, I thank you for your constant and continuous encouragement. To my sister-in-law Regina Kennedy, your brave and kind heart makes you who you are; I applaud your honesty and openness. To families who have experienced domestic abuse and violence, my heart is with you. To my blended family of sons, daughters-in-law, granddaughters, and nieces and nephews, some believe that if it is a man that hurts you, it takes another man to heal you. Or, if it is a woman that hurts or rejects you, it takes another woman to make you forget about it. Remember this: Heavenly hosts will always use what hurts you to heal you. Healing comes through pure love, and pure love does not hurt.

DEDICATION

In loving memory of my Mother: Ada Lee Horn Jefferson,
your DNA has and will always be my strength.
Thank you for giving me life's most precious gift, "Love."

In loving memory of my Sorority Sister, Pheonecia Ratliff,
of Lambda Beta Chapter, Zeta Phi Beta Sorority, Inc.,
you will always be remembered, loved, and missed.

Author Affirmation:

"With man, this is impossible, but with God, all things are possible."
Matthew 19:26 (New International Version)

TABLE OF CONTENTS

FOREWORD

When asking Dr. Lewis why she chose the term "watershed" as a part of her book's title, she paused and carefully explained: Watershed moments are ubiquitous (ever-present); they are universal. However, those global moments experienced by many become a personal universe as felt only by the abused. At that moment, the heart wants to stop, and the soul wants to cry out. Tears lose light and become dark, so dark and hot that they cause wet streaks across one's face. In that watershed moment, you know the only person who has vowed to care for you the most has, in some form, violently and ruthlessly betrayed that vow. Tears of betrayal involve the darkest, hottest, most bitter tears that will ever disturb your soul or touch your face. A partner hitting, kicking, cursing, cheating, lying, humiliating, threatening, raping, or abusing you in some other unforeseen, inexplicable, unexpected, God-forsaken manner is intolerable. It is then that we must pray to our most high God from the depths of our souls and rest assured that our Lord God hears us. I know this is true, for He has heard and answered my prayers many times.

Dark Tears, Light Tears, do not tell someone else how to pray from the depths of the soul, only to have faith and trust. When reading *Dark Tears, Light Tears,* unforgivable, despicable acts of violence frequently became watershed moments, and you find yourself standing at your life's crossroads. Your life's intersection is the place where you have reached the turning point, and you ask yourself, "Which road do I take?" It is then, and only then that you can rest assured there is a higher power that can turn your darkest tears toward the light, tears embraced by a light that shines bright enough to direct your path forever. Now, you have become the watershed; your tears are like that ridge of land, separating the waters. Your soul now separates your dark tears from your light tears. In essence, tears are like waters flowing in different directions, drained from their natural existence by abuse and betrayal, which the depths of your soul can only restore. After reading *Dark Tears, Light Tears*, you will become victorious if you are the victim; if you have experienced domestic violence, you will share your story. If you are the abuser, you will positively reshape your life and the lives of your loved ones. *Dark Tears, Light Tears* tells us that when we approach the crossroads of our lives, it is never too late to change, and never too late for our dark tears to become light because *what man says is impossible; God says it is possible.*

PREFACE

M. C. Albrecht once remarked, "A close relationship exists between an author's personality and his or her creative writings." However, "truth comes essentially from within," and the one indispensable rule to writing a good book is "to have an invincible faith in that which one writes."[1] As a person with first-hand experience as a domestic abuse victim, it was challenging to write about it. With every keystroke, it was a struggle to move forward and keep writing, even though I would see people around me finishing their books. My husband, or someone else I know, would ask me, "Did you ever finish writing that book?" "What is taking so long?" "You know, X finished her book, Y finished her book, and Z published his book." Or, I would hear comments such as, "Didn't they teach you all how to write during all those years you went to school?" Feeling disappointed in myself because I had not finished writing, my heart would become overwhelmed with sadness and disappointment.

In addition to the questions about why I had not finished writing my book, I could hear bits and pieces of what I had written every time I read an article, turned on the TV, listened to a podcast, or watched a broadcast. Then, I would get an email from a publishing company every other day, saying, "Time is running out; publish this week to get your special rate before the special rate goes away."

One day, I sat staring at my computer and contemplating what was taking so long. Aside from this being my first book, I also feared writing something that no one easily understood, worried that no one would want to read it or have stark criticism. But what was it that was keeping me paralyzed? What kept me from writing words on paper about a subject matter that burned so deep inside me? And there they were, teardrops of pain and joy, light and darkness that became eminent as the author wrote. Like shards of glass piercing my soul, I knew abuse was a subject matter that one would rather forget than remember. When I took a second look at the books of X, Y, and Z, and others I knew had written, they dealt with leadership, business, sugar, spice, and pleasant things.

The subject matter in my heart bore unspeakable darkness, and it was a need to write about the one thing that keeps a home from being a peaceful and safe haven. I had suffered physical, mental, psychological, financial, and emotional domestic abuse and violence. However, like a phoenix rising from the ashes, I survived, and others survived domestic abuse and violence. And yes, my Christian faith was instrumental in allowing me to do that. Suffering domestic abuse within the home is a tragedy, but it was not enough to write about the trauma of violence through long or short-term abuse. There is a lack of awareness concerning domestic violence that needs unveiling. Intimate partner abuse has too often been a secret within the community — a deadly secret for victims that may include their children and other family members. More often than not, many women and men hesitate to report their abuse to the police. They may not trust the police or want to see their partners arrested—particularly Black women, who do not want to see their partners become another Black man behind bars.[2]

Consistent, long-term, and short-term checks and balances are needed because domestic abuse and violence have long-standing effects. It impacts our children, parents, sisters, brothers, friends, church members, college roommates, other relatives, and our communities at large: the list is endless. Experiences of domestic abuse, standing alone, may be remarkable: experiences of many are significant, astonishing, and book-worthy. Domestic abuse and violence are actual events affecting both men and women; in fact, it affects us all in one way or another. When intimate partners are abusers, it creates hardships and insurmountable circumstances for their victims. Feeling within a silo; however, victims are never alone. There is always another victim somewhere, too embarrassed or afraid to speak out. The negative impact is unquestionably horrific and ongoing. Deliberate and conscious efforts, which create awareness about the devastating effects of domestic abuse and violence, may save or improve the life of someone we all know and love.

INTRODUCTION

Understand that adult development, at any age, defies embryology. Embryology is a science that deals with human offspring's growth, development, and structure until the second month of life. Anxiety and heartbreak, and its residual tenderness, are far-reaching and in-discriminant. I have found that when entering and passing through individual emotional states of mind, we are not alone. As embryos are a collection of underdeveloped cells before significant human life organs are fully developed, so are emotional strains within us as we grow older. As we age, our selection of intrinsic experiences is similar. Irrespective of genetics, national origin, race, color, religion, sex, or gender identity, the challenge to stay in the middle rather than buy into the struggle and complain (avoiding rigidity and fear) requires maturation. And sometimes, it also involves a sense of letting go, honing self-awareness, and possibly undergoing an identity shift. Carefully protecting an embryo's delicate development--prevents it from being snuffed away; likewise, we must take care of our fragile youth to reach adult development and the aging process.

As we enjoy our later years, we must inform, enlighten, and open our eyes and the next generation. Particularly in the unfortunate circumstances that females (and sometimes males) often face in domestic violence situations. Although we try to shelter our children, grandchildren, and all females and males from the harsh reality of domestic abuse and violence, it is impossible to do so. It would be better for them to have read or listened to the experiences of others than to have similar experiences of their own. For this purpose, the harsh subject matter of domestic abuse and violence becomes necessary to discuss.

Domestic violence is vicious within the home. It may occur between married couples or non-married couples who are living together. Carson and Worden (2005) explained that no single set of words could fully define domestic abuse and violence. However, it is often termed intimate partner violence and committed by one person against the other while in a personal relationship.[1] The ties can be heterosexual, same-sex, a former spouse or partner, a divorcee, or an estranged spouse or partner, meaning you are legally or otherwise separated but not yet divorced. For example, if you are divorced, that is your former spouse or partner. However, if you are separated, that becomes your estranged spouse or partner. In a general sense, domestic violence may involve harm against persons of any age. It occurs in various forms: physical, mental, verbal, emotional, economic, religious, or sexual abuse. It may be elusive or blatant, emerging as marital rape, choking, beating, or another life-threatening encounter.

Before 1973, no one had used the term domestic violence. Jack Ashley coined the term in 1973 when he addressed the Parliament of the United Kingdom—during previous times; it referenced civil unrest or violence within a country or foreign territory rather than violence from another within the home[2]. No one used the term to refer to intimate partners turning on one another. Earlier on, it was associated primarily with physical violence between married couples and referred to as wife-beating or wife-battering. But because violence occurred to more than just the wife, it is now broadly defined to include "all acts of physical, sexual, psychological or economic violence" committed by one intimate partner against the other.[3] Domestic violence can occur against anyone at any age, including children, teenagers, parents, or the elderly. This writing focuses on violence between couples who were married, cohabitated, or non-cohabitating intimate partners. Used interchangeably are the terms domestic violence, domestic abuse, and intimate partner violence. The focus of intimate partner and ex-partner violence in this writing signifies the likelihood of fear, threats, and injury to women instead of men.

In 1991, Ms. Anita Hill, an African-American female, testified during the Senate Judiciary's Committee confirmation hearings of Supreme Court Justice Clarence Thomas. During her testimony, she said it best, ".... there are women and some men now who have just really lost confidence in our government to respond to the problem of gender violence."[4] Ms. Hill's 1991 statement stills hold today. Domestic abuse is not an easy subject matter, and it can be stressful, painful, and disturbing. However, there are no pleasant home abuse experiences, but only abusive experiences that have improved because they did not end worse. Domestic violence is a wicked and spiraling public policy that begins at home and spreads abroad.

The following chapters highlight the true impact of abuse and domestic violence. Chapter One describes the worldwide difficulty associated with resolving domestic abuse and violence. Chapter Two provides a historical perspective, and Chapter Three represents the silencing effect of domestic abuse. Chapter Four describes the interconnection abusive relationships forces all to share. Chapter Five begins the introduction of Anna (her pseudonym chosen for privacy). Anna is an abused woman who shared her background and experience of domestic violence with the author. Chapter Six continues the story of Anna. Chapter Seven through Chapter Eleven describes the abusive relationships endured by five other women who have chosen the pseudonyms Grace, Emma, Corona, Allison, and Nicollette to protect their privacy. The five women, in their own words, share detailed experiences of domestic violence and abuse. Finally, Chapter Twelve describes parallels between light and darkness. When lines are parallel, they run continuously and never meet. Likewise, domestic abuse and sanctity within one's home will never meet.

CHAPTER ONE

A Wicked Problem

According to Pema Chödrön, a Buddhist instructor, "Anxiety, heartbreak, and tenderness marks an in-between state, a place where we consciously or unconsciously want to avoid. However, the challenge is to accept the struggle, not complain, and allow our in-between states to soften us rather than make us rigid and afraid" to face difficulties associated with domestic abuse. [1] The tenderness brought on by years of anxiety and heartbreak from violence and abuse within the home is uncomfortable and frequently painful. However, it brings about an *embryonic-like* condition of adult development and aging. Therefore, our life's journey is a combined total of heaven and earth's transformation. We all have at least one story to tell that may help someone else, so the information and subject matter addressed within this context center on domestic abuse, violence, intimate partner abuse, and its many repercussions.

Search for anything, search for everything. Search social media platforms, view televised documentaries, read any book, magazine, or newspaper, or listen to the radio. Intrinsic and extrinsic struggles are forever present. Our efforts to overcome pain and suffering frequently require a transformation by both heaven and earth, which will produce both *Dark Tears* and *Light Tears*. However, the goal is never to allow someone to be your priority while allowing yourself to be their option.

The chapters that follow address one wicked problem. It spotlights age-old questions concerning domestic abuse and violence, along with one possible resolution—*dark and light tears* of resilience. Highlighted are a few stories, facts, and figures representing the isolation, struggle, and successes of many connected to domestic violence. As previously mentioned, domestic abuse comes in many forms, filled with mental anguish. Whatever the condition, it is an overpowering, reactive, or non-reactive state unimaginable for many, unforgettable for most, and unlikely for a few. However, any abuse within the household between intimate partners, whether married or not married, constitutes a travesty. These forms of abuse, in part, adapted from K. Wilson (2005), are described as followed:[2]

> ***Physical*** *– A mix of assaulting acts designed to humiliate, intimidate, and manipulate an intimate partner to achieve compliance and dependence.*
>
> > *Examples: Kicking, hitting, punching, choking, and stabbing*
>
> ***Mental or Psychological*** *– Pervasive, repeated, and indisputable acts associated with diminished psychological stamina.*
>
> > *Examples: Constant belittlement, harassment, hostile home environment*
>
> ***Verbal*** *– Derogatory words often spoken along with profanity that offends, irritates, agitate, humiliates, and diminishes the self-confidence and self-worth of an intimate partner.*
>
> > *Examples: Excessive cursing and constant name-calling*
>
> ***Emotional*** *– Long or short-term – severe and obtrusive behavior designed to destabilize feelings and reactions of an intimate partner.*
>
> > *Examples: Badgering and humiliation in front of others*

Economical *– The seizing and control of assets by one intimate partner from the other; these assets are needed to maintain and sustain independence and individualism*

Examples: Taking the car or car keys and taking money, locking out of the home

Sexual *– Lewd and disgusting behavior forces a conscious or unconscious partner to participate in unwanted sexual acts, constituting a criminal act*

Notwithstanding the descriptions above, many world events have taken place, which has shattered the sheer fabric of our society: mobs that stormed our US Capitol and mass murders in locations designated as places of religious worship. Shootings in schools, defined as places for learning and growth—marathons, named for developing a sense of community honoring worthy causes, shopping centers, or grocery markets where all should feel safe: all tainted by unsuspecting violence. The heightened importance of loss where shootings occurred in nightclubs, places for meeting others and having fun, or the unthinkable acts that spawned the "Black Lives Matter Movement" cannot be understated. Some purported the Black Lives Matter movement was a political stance forced down the opposing party's throats.[3] Others argued that supporting Black Lives Matter was not partisan nor political.[4] Irrespective of the cause, law enforcement officers have killed Black or African-Americans at a rate twice as high as White Americans, but why this statistic exists is debatable.[5] These violent and terroristic acts are too numerous to make noteworthy in this text. Although the shared stories of pain, suffering, and resilience apportioned a charred and frightening similarity to many forms of violence for which we have all become too familiar.

Within the United States alone, more than ten million people experience domestic violence every year. While there are countless cases not reported each year, there are between 960,000 and 3,000,000 incidents yearly. Moreover, the Violence Policy Center says that a former or romantic partner kills nearly three women every day in the United States within women's homes.[6] Usually, these violent acts occur because the victim wanted to leave the relationship. Although African-American women make up only about 13 percent of all women in the United States, they comprise one-half of all female homicide victims killed by their current or former boyfriend or husband.[7] Domestic violence rates are 35 percent higher for African-American women than Caucasian women.[8] To better understand how to stop the ramifications of domestic abuse and violence, additional education, awareness, and mental health resources are needed.

How long does it take for victims to recognize that their spouse or significant other has a personality or mean streak cut directly from an evil cloth of abuse and violence? What form will it take next when it rears its ugly head? Will it be a slap, a punch, harsh words, the silent treatment, embarrassment in front of others, adultery, intimidation of the children, the forcing from one's home, threats of leaving home, financial punishment? What form will it take, and how long will it last?

Alas, there are more sobering questions, such as how long does it take to heal from such acts? Who can you tell, or where do you go? In other words, can you bear this cross alone? If so, at what price? Be aware the fee collectors will come in this life, not the next. There will be some late nights, some *dark tears,* but, thankfully, some *light tears as well.* There will be some broken hearts, and yes, there will be divorce and even death. But remember, tears endure through the night, but joy comes in the morning. How many more nights and mornings will happen until the victim choose to become victorious *(if ever, which is even more perplexing)?* Will this writing, the dialogue in this book, ignite a more vigorous conversation about domestic violence and abuse? Or, will a *spiral of silence* forever endure?

Domestic abuse and violence have no boundaries. Many researchers have studied risks associated with domestic abuse and resilience, and there is "no single pathway" that leads to a resolution. Many scholars agree remnants of abusive behavior in people are massive. Abuse creates specific and nonspecific drawbacks for the abused. Domestic abuse and violence encouraged reduced levels of family supervision and communication. Reduced family attention and communication commonly lead to conduct problems, delinquency, and substance abuse in children and teenagers. Therefore, alcoholism, depression, shyness, withdrawal, low levels of achievement, hyperactivity, and high levels of disorders related to attention deficits are waiting to happen next in a victim.

Domestic abuse and violence are terrible phenomena wherein at least thirty-eight states within the United States have placed penalties within the criminal code.[9] Most state governments consider domestic abuse a factor when determining custody and visitation of a minor child. While every state in the United States has adopted some form of penalty for domestic abuse and violence, this wicked problem still exists. Domestic abuse and violence are "equal opportunity problems"; there is no divide.

When I first began writing about domestic violence, I wanted to follow what I had learned, narrow my topic, and find a particular demographic set to focus my research. Therefore, the plight of African-American females and domestic violence immediately came to mind. As someone who had suffered abuse as an African-American female, I could quickly identify.

Moreover, the research gathered led me to believe that African-American females were the dominant owners of this form of life happiness—interrupted; nonetheless, I found this untrue. My former statement concerning domestic abuse and violence as an "equal opportunity problem" shows more validity than many others.

During the 2020 COVID-19 pandemic, the imposition of stay-at-home requirements caused a drastic increase in police calls concerning domestic altercations. The United Nations called it a "Shadow Pandemic."[10] The South African President, Cyril Ramaphosa, referred to gender-based violence as the "Second Pandemic."[11] A pandemic unseen, lurking beneath the surface, victims were trapped inside with their abusers, cloaked as caring partners. As stress levels climbed due to extra time spent at home, food insecurities and financial hardships increased, making bad situations worse.

During the 2019 pandemic, the Indiana Coalition against Domestic Violence cited a 113 percent increase in homicides related to domestic violence and counted ten deaths in just one week.[12] The rise in violence began with the stay-at-home orders, followed by a slowed economy, increased access to firearms, and tensions, which created a "perfect storm" for domestic violence. Isolation during the pandemic decreased access to social support systems, which posed a catastrophic setting for individuals struggling with domestic violence. On April 9, 2020, around 3:00 pm, Officer Breann R. Leath was shot and killed while responding to a domestic violence disturbance call. Officer Leath was only 24 years old.[13] During 1996-2010, more than one hundred sixteen police officers were killed in the line of duty while responding to domestic disturbance calls. Perpetrators with firearms killed ninety-five percent of those officers.[14] Officer Leath's death and the death of others exemplify the need to explore narratives associated with intimate partner violence.

Consider the fate of Pheonecia Ratliff, a 23-year-old college senior at Jackson State University, Jackson, MS. A mother to her baby daughter and a beloved member of Zeta Phi Beta Sorority, Inc. In May 2020, after Ms. Ratliff filed domestic violence and stalking charges against Jamarquis Black, her ex-boyfriend, he kidnapped her, shot her sister, and killed her and himself in a murder-suicide on Interstate 55.[15]

Unfortunately, Ms. Ratliff was not the only domestic violence victim at Jackson State University in Jackson, MS. In 2007, Latasha Norman's ex-boyfriend murdered her. He stabbed her in the chest, stuffed her in the trunk of her car, and placed her body in a wooded area in North Jackson in Jackson, MS. Ms. Norman was a 20-year-old Jackson State University student. Since Ms. Norman's death, organizers have held events every year to encourage men and women to speak out concerning domestic violence before it is too late. The University also named a counseling center after Ms. Norman. Nonetheless, domestic violence continues to leave long-term mental and psychological impacts for many men and women.[16]

CHAPTER TWO

How Did We Get Here?

Reflections

As we age, life reflections multiply, and yearly revelations occur. Specific changes relative to how we accept who we are and the actions of others occur through conscious and unconscious decision-making. When we enter a viable relationship, defining moments cause a sense of pivotal and emotional change within us, which induces a subtle, melodic line between knowledge gained and ignorance recognized through one's self-reflection.

Baby-booming Generation

Benjamin Franklin said, "Without continual growth and progress, such words as improvement, achievement, and success have no meaning."[1] Before continuing, it is first necessary to briefly visit a few significant, historical, and formidable events that shaped the decade in which many in this generation were born. In 1946, there were 3.4 million babies born, beginning what later became known as the "baby-booming" generation. This booming birth rate ended in 1964, with a record-setting 77 million "baby boomers." However, there has been a long-standing debate relative to who the "true baby boomers" really are.

Nonetheless, most historians agree that *real baby boomers* share similar characteristics, such as cultural, economic, and social factors. Nearly all agree that the actual baby boomers were born between 1946 and 1955. However, for all intended purposes, baby boomers are classified as born between 1946 and 1964. Baby boomers were beginning to exist when generational writers characterized the 1950s as having a booming economy. The gross national product (GNP) doubled--growing from $200 billion to $500 billion. The government spent money on constructing interstate highways, schools, increasing veterans' benefits, military spending, and technologies such as computers.[2]

When World War II came to an end in 1945, and by the end of the 1950s, America's future was booming and bright. The United States had the world's most reliable military power, where both unemployment and inflation rates were low, and the middle-class people had more money to spend. New cars, suburban houses, and other consumer goods were available to more people than ever reported. However, the 1950s brought about an era of great conflict as well.[3]

Wife-beating

Wife-beating is synonymous with slavery, which slavery began in America around 1619. A privateer vessel, known as the White Lion, seized a Portuguese slave ship, the Sao Jao Bautista, and took twenty African slaves. They brought the slaves ashore to what was known as the British Colony of Jamestown, Virginia. In 1641, within the Massachusetts Bay Colony, a declaration stated married women were free from "bodily [bodilie] correction or stripes by her husband." The 1641 declaration in Massachusetts was called the "Body of Liberties." The Body of Liberties document established the first legal codes that prevented wife-Beating in America. However, scholarly debates continue regarding whether these liberties were ever approved or adopted by the courts. As a sign of authority and power, men were legally allowed to beat their wives as a form of male validation in the household. This legal authority of wife-beating lasted until the mid-1800s.[4]

In 1850, Tennessee was the first state in the United States to outlaw wife-beating officially. Also, during the 1800s, there was the Civil War, with the fight between the northern states (Union) or anti-slavery states, loyal to the United States, and the southern states (Confederate States of America), those dedicated to slavery. The Northern States included California, Connecticut, Delaware, Illinois, Indiana, Iowa, Kentucky, Maine, Maryland, Massachusetts, Michigan, Minnesota, Missouri, New Hampshire, New Jersey, New York, Ohio, Oregon, Pennsylvania, Rhode Island, Vermont, and Wisconsin. Kansas, Nevada, and West Virginia joined the northern states during the Civil War. The Confederate or southern States included Alabama, Arkansas, Florida, Georgia, Louisiana, Mississippi, North Carolina, South Carolina, Tennessee, Texas, and Virginia. The Civil War lasted from 1861 until 1865. In 1865, Robert E. Lee, a Confederate general in the Civil War, surrendered at Appomattox, Virginia. After his defeat and surrender in the Battle of Fort Sumter, slavery ended.[5] On September 22, 1862, President Abraham Lincoln signed a preliminary Emancipation Proclamation, which declared that all enslaved people would be declared forever free as of January 1, 1863.[6] However, it was not until June 19, 1865, that enslaved Americans in Galveston, Texas, learned of the proclamation. On June 18, 2021, Joseph R. Biden Jr., President of the United States of America, Proclaimed June 19, 2021, as Juneteenth Day of Observance, which acknowledged and officially celebrated the end of the Civil War and the Emancipation of Black Americans within the United States.[7]

In 1878, the United Kingdom declared it legal for a wife to separate from an abusive husband, and within the United States, the claimed rights of husbands to beat their wives were no longer a valid claim. However, during the early 1900s, there were very few recourses for a woman abused by her husband. Wife-beating aligns with a slave mentality.[8]

In 1993, the United Nations published *Strategies for Confronting Domestic Violence: A Resource Manual.* Within that resource manual, it urged countries to cite domestic violence as a criminal offense. It also acknowledged that the right to privacy in the home should not include the right to abuse a family member and further recognized that the old legal system had considered domestic violence outside the scope of the law. It specifically stated the following: Physical discipline of children is allowed and, indeed, encouraged in many legal systems, and a large number of countries allow moderate physical chastisement of a wife or, if they do not do so now, have done so within the last 100 years. Most legal systems failed to criminalize circumstances where a wife undergoes force to have sexual relations with her husband against her will. In the case of violence against wives, there is a widespread belief that women provoke, can tolerate, or even enjoy a certain level of violence from their spouses.[9]

Historical Conflict

More than 350,000 women served in the US Armed Forces during World War II or had jobs outside the home because many men were fighting in the war, and women fulfilled roles that did not require physical combat. However, when the war ended, and families moved to the suburbs, women were urged to leave the workforce, stay home, and bear and rear children. Betty Friedan, a noted feminist advocate, equated this notion to an act of "*burying women alive*." As women left the workforce to stay home, feminist rights movements began, as many women were dissatisfied with staying home and continually yearned for a more fulfilling way of life.[10]

Civil Rights Movement

Along with the feminist movement, the fight against inequality and injustice for African-Americans was underway. However, it was not until 1954 that the Civil Rights movement became mainstream and entered the American way of life. In 1954, the Supreme Court declared that "separate educational facilities" for black children were "inherently unequal." Brown v. Board of Education's landmark case caused an uprising in the south, as Whites resisted the Brown ruling. As segregation was stoutly defended by some Whites, in December 1955, Rosa Parks, an African-American female and Civil Rights activist from Montgomery, Alabama, was arrested for refusing to give up her seat on a city bus to a White person. Rosa Parks' arrest sparked massive, nonviolent protests, such as boycotts in public places and public services; however, it also ignited great civil unrest, which shaped the Civil Rights movement and created practices of civil liberties for decades to come.[11]

CHAPTER THREE

SPIRAL OF SILENCE

"For I will restore health unto thee, and I will heal thee of thy wounds, saith the Lord."

Jeremiah 30:17

Is Silence Golden?

The adage of "silence is golden" in a pattern of domestic abuse is of no value. How many times does anyone need to ask, "Why didn't we know about this?" In 1974, a German political scientist, Elisabeth Noelle Neumann, developed a theory to explain public opinion on morally or politically loaded subject matter. According to Ms. Neumann, public opinion is the "attitudes one can express without running into the danger of isolating oneself."[1] The term *spiral of silence* refers to the pressure felt when there is a need to hide how a person truly feels when they believe their opinion is of the minority--because the majority will not accept the person's feelings about a controversial subject matter.[2] Contentious subject matter includes debates associated with the right to possess semi-automatic firearms, stand your ground legislation, and police brutality. It can consist of arguments related to punishment about Catholicism and pedophilia, immigration policies, abortion legislation, domestic violence punishment, fault, and policy.

Anyone discussing or amplifying trials and tribulations associated with domestic abuse and violence or other contentious topics with others risk stigmatizing a person with an unwanted label. This stigma, shame, or disdain creates a fear of being isolated or ostracized, which produces a "*bandwagon effect*" for the person. Who jumps on the bandwagon, actively supporting what they believe is a more fashionable or popular opinion? Possibly, religious congregations favor the majority's opinion while forsaking their own beliefs about pro-life or a woman's right to choose (pro-choice) topics relative to abortion. Politicians may join the bandwagon, flying flags labeled with plans of what's in it for me rather than their constituents. Perhaps included are workers or co-workers seeking a promotion, managers seeking senior management positions, an associate who wants to be an assistant or an assistant who wants to be "the director, etc.? Because all want cohesion and acceptance, we seek approval and recognition from others. Those who overwhelmingly join the bandwagon of public opinion, irrespective of the controversial topic, will forego their voice or opinion and accept the vote or opinion of the perceived majority. Sometimes, and in most instances, this overwhelming need for support and acceptance causes more harm than good.

But, how do we know whether our opinion is a part of the minority or the majority? Well, we all have a sixth sense. Remember the 1999 movie "*Sixth Sense*" directed by M. Night Shyamalan, starring Bruce Willis as a troubled child psychologist and Haley Joel Osment as an anxious, isolated boy. The boy was upset and lonely. In the movie, he could see and talk to dead people; however, no one wanted anything to do with the boy except for the lone psychologist, who tried to help him. He happened to be equally as troubled because he was dead himself and did not know it (as you learn at the movie's end). How confusing was that? In essence, a domestic abuser is killing his own family in his own home and doesn't even know it. By staying in that situation for whatever the reason might be, the victim is trying to help but can't because she (or he) is slowly dying inside themselves.

Fictional movies are one thing, but non-fictional life is another. In reality, Elisabeth Noelle-Neumann believed that everyone has a "quasi-statistical sense." Quasi-statistical means that people assume they can sense and figure out what others are thinking. This quasi-statistical sense allows individuals, such as church attendees, politicians, or voters, to examine their social environments and gauge which opinions are more popular or gaining the most support. The perceived popular view influences the willingness to remain silent or a willingness to speak out about controversial issues, such as domestic abuse and violence, how to vote, or whether to impeach a president (twice), for that matter.

Even better, let's take a brief look at the 2016 presidential election results and beyond. American media outlets expended more energy on former President Donald Trump than any other president in American history. During 2016, the debate seemed to be never-ending regarding whether candidate Donald Trump would win the election or candidate Hillary Clinton. Yet, polls, pundits, and experts all got it wrong. Why?

It was simple; no one wanted to say out loud that they would vote for candidate Donald Trump because the vast majority may have perceived their choice as unpopular. So, they kept their opinions hidden. Even the director of the University of Virginia's Center of Politics stated about the election outcome:

We were wrong. The entire punditry industry, the entire polling industry, the entire analyst industry – and I want to use this opportunity to take my fair share of the blame – we were wrong," "We, the whole industry, have a lot to learn from this." "How do you capture people who maybe won't talk to pollsters or will fib to pollsters?" "It's an industry-wide failure, and we've got to get it fixed. This election was a spectacular event that we will be studying for the rest of our lives.[3]

Yet, that director never once mentioned the Spiral of Silence Theory. Elisabeth Noelle-Neumann, a Professor for Communication Research at the University of Mainz and Director of the Public Opinion Research Center in Germany, observed the 1980 U. S. Presidential election between President Jimmy Carter and his opponent Ronald Reagan. As told by the news media, the power of public opinion should have drastically swayed the outcome of the election. During the election, voting intentions, according to the news media, were reported for both sides. The press had been active, convincing the mass to accept what appeared to be favorable public opinions for the Democratic party. However, the outcome of the election was unexpected. What happened? The majority's perceived views had effectively silenced others' genuine opinions, fearing that the perceived majority would be dissatisfied with actual views. Noelle-Neumann argued that if pollsters had asked voters who do you plan to vote for instead of who do you think will win the election, there would have been a correct forecasted outcome. Likewise, if we ask, are you, or have you been a victim of domestic abuse? Instead of asking, do you believe persons are domestic abuse victims, perhaps we could better assist the victims? A *spiral of silence* develops as abuse victims' voices become marginalized. A small number of opinions frequently shared across many different venues becomes the dominant opinion.

Soon, many people start to share common values, and their actions or interests represent those opinions. When this happens, those in the shared group or reference group seek recognition and acceptance from others. The recognition and acceptance become so important that some are willing to remain silent when they know what they are thinking or doing is wrong—this spiral of silence leads others to stay quiet despite their true beliefs. Domestic abuse incidents are sensitive and similar to voter pressure. Both occurrences can induce a fear of isolation, thereby creating a perpetual spiral of silence. Like other controversial acts or topics, experiences of domestic abuse, violence, and plain maltreatment are far-reaching and indiscriminate.

Religious Impact

Religion plays a significant role in the lives of many individuals. For African-American women, the *Black Church* and faith and the religious community function as the framework for guidance, proper conduct, and attitudinal developments about marriage, divorce, and relationships overall. Thus, the sacred (*Black Church*) framework has caused African-American women to negotiate their safety away from their abusers for acceptance among church congregations. Seeking this level of acceptance evades spiritual growth and has caused African American Females to operate within a more traditional worldview of marriage and divorce expectations within the church. The Pew Research Center showed that 53 percent of African-Americans attend church every week. Research indicates that Clergy underestimates the number of victims of domestic violence within the church and infrequently addresses this problem from the pulpit. Moreover, attempting to address the problem may worsen matters because couples' counseling may fail to assess safety risks properly.[4]

Additionally, African-American women have more significant religious commitments than white women, Hispanic women, and African-American men. Women who told their stories for this text prayed to

God for help with their abusive situations. Their mention of prayer for relief is consistent with the national norm that says 80 percent of all African-American women firmly believe that religion is essential in their lives.[5] Furthermore, they believe that prayer has helped them with facing their abusive relationships and situations. Nonetheless, irrespective of race, churchgoers share cohesive beliefs formed early in life as a reference group. The shared belief is that prayer made a positive difference in their lives when facing the adversities concerning domestic violence.

As a part of the conceptual spiral of silence, African-American women continue to condone concepts of the majority about not getting a divorce, despite their disagreement with the re-occurrence of domestic abuse and violence in relationships. There are ongoing debates among many about whether religious individuals should be neutral and not participate or speak out on controversial issues regarding the institution of marriage, divorce, domestic abuse, and violence. The notion that religious individuals should be neutral has created a *fear of isolation* among some parishioners. Fear is a powerful emotion; it controls our behavior and either unites or divides our connections to others.[6]

Those who fear isolation sacrifice their true beliefs because their ideas may not match the perceived expectations of the majority of their counterparts. For example, at eight years old, Anna (as shared in chapter 6) was expected to sit on the front pew (mourner's bench) and pray to have her soul purged from eternal damnation. However, most of the time, she was too hungry to pray and wondered if she would starve to death before her soul ever knew what happened. If she did not sit on the mourner's bench, or her older sisters and brothers were not seated there at their appointed times, her family and mother, in particular, would have been seen as outcasts within the congregation. Anna's mother had been sexually assaulted before Anna's conception and knew of Anna's hunger and distress. However, her mother felt compelled to follow tradition within the church. Anna would be required to sit on the mourner's bench. Her mother remained silent about the sexual assault suffered by perhaps a church attendee. Outcasts among churchgoers are synonymous with the fear of isolation and a willingness to speak out about unfavorable occurrences and the perceived impact among the majority.

To assist those dealing with domestic abuse problems, communication within the church should not be elusive, obtrusive, conclusive, or judgmental, but relatively transparent, open, tangible, descriptive, non-judgmental, and unbiased. Leadership begins and ends in the pulpit, so principles disseminated from the pulpit guide the thought processes of the congregation and, ultimately, come back to the primary church leader through unwanted or unexpected consequences. Consequences include declining or poor church attendance, a lack of church participation through service, or monetary contributions.

To improve the overall experience of African-American women at home, within the church, and in the community, attitudinal shifts and self-awareness deserve more profound commitments, and involvement is needed. Involvement might include providing additional resources such as workshops or training for clergy about the implications of domestic violence. A desirable outcome can come from proper communication between church leaders and followers. Masking and causal connections create internal and external injury for individuals and groups and are irreparable. Seeking professional assistance from mental health organizations or social worker volunteers would lessen damage to individuals and those within the church and the community.[7]

Surviving sufferings brought about through tumultuous domestic abuse and violence requires innate positivity. As survivors of abuse, many have lived through countless hardships and watershed moments. They have closed the gap and crossed the bridge of both "dark tears and light tears"; and, for the most part, through life or death. An abused woman is a brave woman who deserves a life where she is no longer a victim but victorious. Eradication of domestic violence and abuse rests upon the spine of the country as a whole. The voices of those who cry out from the cracks within our walls should not be marginalized but heard, believed, and protected.

CHAPTER FOUR

THE GREAT DIVIDE OR IS IT?

To better understand the level of domestic abuse that continues to plague our homes to date, 147 participants volunteered and responded to a short survey about domestic abuse administered by the author. Income for participants of the study ranged from $0 to $200,000+. The majority of the participants in this survey's annual income ranged from $50,000-$74,999. The majority of the survey participants also lived in the South Atlantic region of the United States. All survey participants were volunteers and participated in the survey using IOS phones, tablets, android phones or tablets, other phones or tablets, Windows desktops or laptops, MacOS desktops or laptops.

Survey findings were astonishing. The responses suggested a growing and changing dynamic concerning domestic abuse and violent behavior within the home. The results were precise. Most survey participants had experienced domestic abuse and continued to suffer from its mental consequences at an alarming rate.

For some, domestic abuse experiences often began in early childhood. The exposure came in many different forms. It may have been physical (slapping, kicking, punching, spitting on the victim, etc.) or mental abuse with cursing and name-calling, deliberately fabricating untruthful events about the victim to family and friends, church members, etc. It may have begun with lived experiences due to infighting of parents, or incestuous acts committed by relatives, or abuse by perceived friends. Domestic abuse may have started with controlling the victims' actions, even attempting to control their thoughts or how they responded to questions posed by others. In some instances, victims were placed on punishment like children and given silent treatment by their abusers. Some victims reported having their car keys hidden or their battery cables unplugged in their cars to prevent them from leaving home. In nearly all the cases, once the abuse began, victims reported the abuse as ongoing and continuous with brief or intermittent periods where the abuser would be kind and apologetic, promising never to abuse the victim again.

Abuse can manifest at any time during a relationship, while some victims reported staying in an abusive relationship for as long as fifteen years. During this writing, some women did not want to be interviewed or participate in the survey because they were still with the abuser or abusive relationship. Numerous women reported that they had a family member or knew of someone in an abusive relationship. When asked why those in abusive relationships continued to stay in the relationship, responses varied. Most survey participants stayed because they had children; other women stayed because they did not have a father growing up and did not want to raise their children without a father in the home. Some stayed because of love for the abuser, while others stayed because of religious beliefs such as, in the eyes of God, they could only have one husband. One victim reported staying in her abusive relationship because she believed that God wanted her to save the abuser from himself. Sacrificing yourself or your children for your own private "higher purpose" does not necessarily make you a firm believer; it could show, on the other hand, a lack in your understanding of true spirituality.

While not all participants chose to respond to all questions, a total of 147 participants ranging in age from 18 to 65 years participated. There were 99 females, 47 males, and one participant who chose not to self-identify. Because some participants elected not to respond to all questions, response totals varied for some questions.

The majority of the survey participants were White or Caucasian (63.01 percent, n=92). Although the Bureau of Statistics tells us that African-American women's domestic violence rates are 35 percent higher than Caucasian women, African-American females were not the majority sample population who chose to participate. There could be several reasons for this; however, there is a possibility that the spiral of silence is alive and well among the African-American population concerning domestic abuse and violence.

The findings showed that all participants in the survey experienced domestic abuse in one form or the other. At least seventy-five participants experienced one or more abuse categories. Emotional abuse occurred most frequently, followed by verbal abuse, mental abuse, and physical abuse, respectively. Twenty-seven percent of the participants stated that they had suffered verbal, physical, mental, and emotional abuse, and 31 percent of the respondents indicated that they had experienced domestic abuse from their parents as children, from other relatives, or in a different category not identified.

When asked the length of time spent in their abusive relationships, participants spent one month to ten years or more in a relationship with their abusers. Survey participants, on average, spent five years in an abusive relationship. Sadly, of the 147 participants, forty-three participants or 29 percent, remained in their abusive relationships when they responded to the survey.

Participants remained in abusive relationships for various reasons. The most substantial reason for staying was love, followed by children, family other than the children, finances, and religious beliefs. One hundred and twenty (120) of the 147 survey respondents stated they had experienced emotional problems, such as anxiety, depression, irritability, or sadness. Of those 120 respondents, twenty-seven participants said they had been highly bothered by anxiety, depression, irritability, or sadness. Thirty stated they had been very disturbed by anxiety, depression, irritability, or despair; eighteen stated they had not been so concerned with anxiety, depression, irritability, or sadness. Sixteen stated no bother at all. Nine said they had suffered some other way not listed on the survey.

Participants also responded to whether there had been abusive warning signs from the abuser that went unnoticed or perhaps ignored at the outset of the relationship. Findings showed all participants in the survey experienced warning signs of domestic abuse in one form or another. Alarmingly, 100 percent, or 147 participants, identified at least two or more perceived warning signs of a potentially abusive relationship while in their relationship. Examples of vicious warning signs include extremely controlling behavior, short or extreme temper tantrums, verbal abuse, and acute jealousy. Also, blaming the victim for anything wrong or bad that happened in the relationship, mood swings, or unpredictable behavior had significance. The belief that a woman should have a lesser role in the relationship than the man, or forced sex, was among the responses received.

Approximately forty-eight participants stated their abusers publicly or privately demeaned, embarrassed, or humiliated them. Forty-five participants said their abusers exhibited extreme jealousy and falsely accused them of flirting with others or having an affair. Another forty-five participants stated their abusers showed extremely controlling behavior by telling them what to wear and ordering them about where or where not to go. All other participants said their abusers handled all the finances to where they had no control of any finances, further showing that they had to ask or beg for any money to spend, even if they had jobs outside the home. Some participants stated their abusers had antiquated beliefs about the roles of women and men in relationships. Nearly all participants said they had experienced all warning signs noted in the survey.

Furthermore, many shared that their abusers insisted they do all the housework in the relationships: cooking (never being late with meals, never burning anything, ensuring that the pancakes were crisp around the edges, etc.), sweeping, mopping (on hands and knees, when ordered), washing, ironing (clothing, bed coverings, drapes, etc.), taking out the garbage, and taking care of the children. Participants stated that their abusers sabotaged or obstructed their ability to work or attend school and isolated them from friends and family members. At least twenty-four participants said their abusers forced them to have sex and disregarded their unwillingness to have sex. Some participants suffered such extreme abusive conditions that they didn't describe it and stated the survey was not adequate to describe what their experiences had been.

Abuse, cloaked in a concept discovered during this writing by the author, is the *creeping compromise,* defined as small, repeated, continuous acts of unkindness that a victim ignores, overlooks, or accepts before the onset and exhibition of concrete forms of domestic abuse and violence. It may begin as what appears as a teasing accusation, such as, for example, "I saw you looking at that man or woman." It could start as questions about interactions with co-workers, friends, or family. It may begin with a simple snatch, push, or pull, a playful slap. It may be severe mood swings, nice or nasty, for no apparent reason. Irrespective of how minor the actions may seem, if it makes the victim uncomfortable and there is a gut feeling that "something is just not right" about this form of treatment, more likely than not, the behavior or actions require questioning or reprimanding attention. Compromising away the more minor things that are upsetting or hurtful rather than addressing them right away leads to larger, more complex problems with no foreseeable solutions. More significant examples of abuse included cursing or slapping victims in public or threatening to drive the car off a bridge and leaving their children for the grandparents to raise. Stabbing victims, putting a loaded or unloaded gun to the heads of victims, forcing victims out of bed in the middle of the night and refusing to allow them to go back to sleep for no reason at all, or forcing victims to engage in sexual acts as a power-play, are also warning signs of abuse.

In addition to those willing to participate in the survey, six participants shared their lived experiences with domestic abuse. The six participants, identified as *Watershed Survivors of Domestic Abuse* because their decisions determined significant turning points that, more likely than not, saved their lives, and the dark and light tears shed paved the way for others. It begins with the lived experiences told about Anna, followed by Grace, Emma, Corona, Allison, and Nicollette as they share their experiences in their own words with the author.

Grace seemed to have been struggling not to relive the events as she spoke about them. Emma evoked passion as she appeared to relive each traumatic moment. She told her story intensely and breathed sighs of relief. Corona had an aura of devout strength about her. She had a quiet demeanor, and although she reflected on the past, it was clear she lived in the present. Her body language oozed with sincerity, honesty, and passion. The domestic abuse she had experienced was as authentic as the air we breathe. Allison agonized; she had paid a high price to try and find love. Any peace that lived within Allison was a true testament to her bravery, and she struggled to find light during her darkest days. Nicolette was majestic. Although scarred, it was clear Nicolette was a survivor. She was firm but not abrasive; secure in her own right; kind, but not weak. Honestly, Nicolette was a force of reckoning who wanted a stable, non-abusive relationship that most, if not all, women deserve.

All the women were brave, their hearts were open, and although they had scars that would last a lifetime, they were willing to share their experiences to help someone else.

CHAPTER FIVE

INTRODUCING ANNA

"For what the law could not do in that it was weak through the flesh, God did by sending His own Son..."

Romans 8:3 (Kings James Version)

A true believer in a higher power more significant than any human could ever imagine, Anna Cutters stood, lost in thought, gazing out of window as she watched the sunset over Lake Michigan. Anna was a pure introvert with a quiet demeanor, frequently perceived as standoffish or cold. But those who knew Anna best loved her and knew that she had a caring heart.

Peace Angel

Peace Angel:

Anna's office, filled with majestic, modern, black-and-white ivory and glass furniture, was priceless. Her office furniture--donated by The Zeiss Museum of Contemporary African Art in Cape Town made the generous furniture donation to Anna's Foundation, Environmental Everglades. Should Anna's foundation cease to exist, this exclusive furniture would go back to the museum. Anna's foundation had built a premier, safe, secure, and uncompromised domestic abuse shelter in an undisclosed location. During the early construction stages of the domestic abuse shelter, the contractors discovered a statue that closely resembled the Angel of Peace at Fatima.

The Angel of Peace appeared to three shepherd children in 1916, which was the same year, Anna's grandmother was born. The angel appeared as "a light, whiter than snow, transparent, and brighter than crystal pierced by the rays of the sun." The Angel of Peace told the children not to be afraid, kneeled, and prayed with them, saying, "My God, I believe, I adore, I hope, and I love you. I ask pardon of you for those who do not believe, do not adore, do not hope, and do not love you." God sent this Angel to sustain Jesus during Jesus' crucifixion. This Angel magnetized the flames of peace, power, healing, truth, faith, and hope. The light and the presence of the Angel of Peace were so powerful. It caused his body to bring forth total momentum and light that he could withstand the betrayal, the trial, and his crucifixion.[1]

The Zeiss Museum Board and its subsidiaries were amazed by Anna's accomplishments and breathtaking generosity. The atmosphere Anna's organization offered included a peaceful sanctuary and haven for the abused. Services provided by Anna's organization were unlike any others the Zeiss Museum officials had ever encountered. The museum willingly donated the furniture for Anna's organization and the statue's transport and preservation.

The Environmental Everglades was effective and efficient. Its primary purpose was to transform the lives of abused, homeless, struggling women, mothers, and daughters by offering sanctity, healing, employment, housing, and educational opportunities. Anna knew that if she overcame her humble beginnings in life, so could others. She attributed her accomplishments to her inconceivable spiritual interactions at the tender age of eight while praying for a more in-depth and better understanding.

***The Baptism*:**

When Anna was eight years old, her family attended a small, one-room, white-structured building called Christian Valley Church. In the small town of Coatopa in Sumter County, Alabama, Christian Valley Church was the religious sanctuary for its rural, primarily indigent, sharecropping, African-American community. Every year, all sinners (non-baptized attendees) sat on the front pew (mourners' bench) during the fall of every year. Sitting on the mourners' bench, they were to pray and ask God to save their souls from eternal damnation. They were to pray without ceasing, of course, while attending church and not attending church. They were to pray continuously during what was known as the season of revival.

At eight years old, Anna was terrified of burning in hell for the rest of her afterlife. However, the most fantastic thing was when she thought back to her childhood; most of the saved adults, who were not sinners and sitting in those other seats, were still fighting their demons. Some of those demons made Sodom and Gomorrah look like the proverbial lily growing in the valley. Admittedly, Anna did not know that prostitution, incest, child abuse, spousal abuse, adultery, and animal cruelty were just a few of the demons making grown-ups and children alike shed dark tears of despair. Moreover, what would she know about that? She was a sinful eight-year-old required to sit on the mourner's bench until she received a sign from God that her soul was free from eternal damnation. And, after receiving that sign, she would be required to shake the hand of any adult who would listen while she sang out her freedom from eternal damnation song:

> *"I'm so glad I got Jesus, I asked the Lord to let me see a leaf on a tree tremble, and he did it, just as sure as I am born."*

Once, she sang the song of acceptance to anyone that would listen, while she held their hand, swinging it back and forth, she could get off that mourners' bench. Anna's total emersion in a body of water (pond) washed all her sins away from the time she was born, or eight years old, until infinity. According to the right hand of fellowship at the Sumter County Christian Valley Church, Anna was now and forever as pure as the white, driven snow, which was "under the right hand of what was known as fellowship," traditionally bestowed upon those baptized at Christian Valley Church.

The ghostly, religious fears instilled in her before, during, and after the age of eight, at times, continuously torment Anna until this very day. Anna remembered that she sat on that mourner's bench and prayed for understanding. She had heard the Great Reverend Medal shout over and over, "In all thy getting, get understanding." She knew that she did not understand any of the things happening in her young life, but she wanted to. She wanted so desperately to understand life itself. She prayed for understanding and believed understanding could surpass and fix everything else that she thought to be wrong at eight years old.

Anna's mother, Adeline, was a strong, God-fearing woman who had raised ten children alone most of her life. Anna's mother's husband died from an unknown cause, leaving Anna's mother alone with seven children. Anna, her sister Deanna, and her brother Todd were born after Anna's mother's husband's death. Their father was not married to Anna's mother. Anna never knew her father and did not believe that Deanna, Todd, nor she had the same father. Anna's conception and birth were difficult times for Anna's mother, though her mother said that Anna was a "gift from God" and that "what the devil had meant for bad had all turned out to be nothing but good." At the wrong hands of her father, Anna's mother, Adeline, was raped.

Although Anna had been a victim of incest as a child and raped as a teenager, she was not aware of the impact it must have had on her life. Relatives assaulted both Anna and her sister Deanna. At an early age, Anna's mother taught her to just move forward despite whatever obstacles faced. Anna did not have many childhood memories, and most memories centered on something she feared. Anna surmised that she was conceived through fear because Anna grew up in a single-parent home. Although Adeline conceived Anna through rape, Adeline loved Anna, and Anna never doubted Adeline's love for one moment. Anna never knew her father; she had only heard rumors and speculations about who he may have been.

When Anna was younger, people said she often spoke whatever came to mind. But, in reality, she was fearful and only spoke after something had bothered her so long that she could no longer hold it inside. Most of the time, it was to correct an injustice that someone other than herself might have been suffering. Anna was unsure where this line of thinking originated but reasoned it must have had something to do with being the youngest of siblings in a large, primarily impoverished family. Anna recalled that sometimes it seemed like so many people were eating at her house, the older siblings would forget to give her food or a chance to eat. Therefore, at an early age, Anna's feelings were feelings of being left out or being put last.

Anna recalled being five years old and clearly remembered the place, even the approximate time of day, her first abuser committed incestuous acts upon her, and precisely how it felt. She recalled the person's bodily fluids and how revolting she thought the actions and fluids were; even as a child, it sickened her to think about it. It was painful, the details nearly unbearable.

As the dark tears flowed from Anna's eyes, she recalled the acts she suffered were nothing compared to those her sister Deanna endured, and she felt lucky for herself and sad for Deanna. Anna hated what was happening, and at the tender age of five, she told an older sister, Dana. She said to Dana that another family member "is doing something to Deanna and me at night." Just five years old, Anna did not know or could not understand what was happening to them, but her greatest fear was that it would never stop. At five years old, she knew what happened made her feel weak, sick, and alone. After telling Dana, the almost nightly lewd acts involving her and Deanna stopped. At least they ended for her and did not happen to Deanna in her presence any longer.

As Anna's teenage years progressed and the older sisters and brothers moved away from home, Anna, Deanna, and a younger nephew, Peter, lived at home with Adeline. Eventually, Deanna lived with an older sister because Anna's oldest brother, Josh, who lived at his mother's house, was an alcoholic. Years before, when Josh went off to college, someone put something in his drink at a nightclub. Whatever someone put in Josh's glass made him lose his mind and, subsequently, placed him in a mental institution. After leaving the mental institution, Josh began to drink heavily; thus, he became an alcoholic who drank profusely during the weekends. Each time Anna and Adeline visited Josh in the mental institution, Anna would beg Adeline to take him out and bring him home. Adeline, who loved her son dearly, followed Anna's advice and took him back home.

Looking back, Anna and Adeline realized it had been a big mistake. On the weekends, Josh would get drunk, remove all his clothes, and walk through the house naked. Somehow, Anna did not feel threatened by

Josh, but Deanna was frightened out of her mind because she believed Josh would soon attempt to assault her sexually. Therefore, Anna's best friend and sister, Deanna, whom she had slept side by side with growing up, played with and suffered through incest with, went to live with their oldest sister, Elma, in another state.

Anna wanted to go too, but because she did not feel threatened by her alcoholic brother, Anna could not live with Elma. Besides, Adeline needed to keep Anna at home to care for her nephew Peter and cook for Josh while Adeline worked continuously. Because Adeline was such a strong, fearfully religious woman, Anna never discussed sex with her mother. Anna had always depended on Deanna, who had gone to live in another state, for that discussion.

So, as a teenager, when Anna became a victim of rape, she had no one to tell. When Anna was in Junior High School, Adeline could not drive and did not have a driver's license. Therefore, Adeline sent Anna to the University of Southern Mississippi to attend driver education classes provided by the University for high school students. Because Anna had to ride the bus to the university, she would have to wait alone at the bus stop. While standing at the bus stop, a 25-year older man named James Boyd approached Anna, offering her a ride and a chance to get out of the pouring rain. He told Anna he knew her family, and he had watched how well she had performed during her driving lessons. Mr. Boyd convinced Anna to get into his shiny red car with the lovely gold rims. Anna clearly remembered her rapist, the shape of his face, the slight twist of his mouth, and the false sense of caring and security he had given her. He raped her more than once. The details, Anna recalled, were painful to remember; they were gruesome and brought back thoughts about her sickening childhood--incestuous assaults and sexual abuse.

Anna recalled the painful days of bleeding that followed the rape and staying in bed for several days, telling Adeline she was too sick to go to school. Anna was an excellent student, so her mother did not question her when she said she was too ill to attend school. Anna never reported the rape, thinking that it would be too much for Adeline to bear. Adeline worked tirelessly and had raised all her children alone. Besides, Adeline still worked as a housekeeper. She did not have much time to concentrate on Anna's problems because she had housekeeping responsibilities for another family for more than eight hours each day. Caring for the family, the Reid family, was essential to Anna's mom, as it had been for Anna's grandmother Lois and her great-grandmother Eunice. Adeline worked at the Reid family's home before Anna ever went to elementary school. She would hide Anna in one of the closets near the kitchen to keep an eye on Anna as she cleaned the Reid family's kitchen and cooked their three meals every day. After the Reid family finished eating, Adeline would gather the leftovers, feed some to Anna, and take the rest home to provide food for the family. Anna enjoyed the cold, homemade, southern sweet tea Adeline made the most. Adeline would take the cold, sugary tea leftover in the glasses, pour it in a glass container, and let Anna drink as much sweet tea as she wanted. Today, Anna hardly ever drinks cold tea; when she does, it's nearly always unsweetened, or she drinks a cup of hot tea with a bit of lemon and honey.

Except for the sweet tea and leftover grits and eggs, the closet experiences were traumatic for Anna. Most times, Anna sat in the closet in the dark so that no one would notice she was there. To this day, Anna is afraid of the dark and has to leave a light on, preferably the closet light. Anna thought it best to heed what she learned during her earlier years: "Just move on." Anna survived her teenage years, managed her way through high school, and went off to college. Indeed, she had been baptized not only in the name of the Father, Son, and the Holy Spirit but the seemingly unholy spirits of life's difficult circumstances.

CHAPTER SIX

PRIORITY OR OPTIONS

"Vows"

I take thee
To be my wife (or husband)
To have and to hold
From this day forward
For better, for worse
For richer, for poorer,
In sickness and in health,
To love and to cherish,
Till death do us part.
According to God's holy law;
And this is my solemn vow.

The Journey Continues

Late British Prime Minister Winston Churchill once said, "The farther backward you can look, the farther forward you can see."[1] Adeline, Anna's mother, and Todd, Anna's brother, took Anna to school for her first day of college. Anna had never been away from her mother's house and away from home for an extended time, except for the two summers she spent in New York with Dana as a pre-teen. After her initial fears of being in college and on her own, and her tears stopped, after watching her mother and brother, Todd, walk away from campus, Anna felt alone. Anna was adamant that she would attend Jackson State University in Jackson, MS, which her sister Deanna attended. However, by the time Anna made it to college and reunited with Deanna, it was Deanna's last year of college. Deanna graduated from college at the end of Anna's freshmen year. Now at college, surrounded by strangers, Anna was, once again, more lost without the comfort of Deanna. Anna was the youngest of all her siblings, so she was the last to leave her mother's house. Anna did not have money but could get a student job, grants, and loans to supplement her tuition and college living expenses.

Anna recalled that the school was going to put her out of college because she needed $75.00. Anna's mother did not have $75.00, and Anna's sister told her to return home. When the weekend came, Anna went home. That same brother, who was a weekend drunk, worked every day during the week as a day laborer. He never spent much money during the week; he only spent money during the weekend on prostitutes and alcohol. He gave Anna $75.00 so she could remain in college. A few years after her brother passed away from a massive heart attack, Anna went through old papers left in his room and found his oldest "*bank book*," a record of his deposits and withdrawals when he first started working as a day laborer. And there it was; he had a total of $150.00 in the bank. Seventy-five dollars had been withdrawn and given to Anna, leaving her brother with only $75.00. Anna's heart filled with both joy and sorrow because he gave her money that he barely had.

One day, feeling alone, and after an economics class ended, Anna met Cornelius. With a broad smile and distinguished eyes, Cornelius approached Anna and said, "Don't I know you?" After meeting Cornelius, Anna remembered staring at him through her dorm window and thinking that he may not be a suitable match for her, but quickly brushed those thoughts aside. Anna later learned that Cornelius's family, like her own, lived far below the poverty level for the number of brothers and sisters in the household and that Cornelius's mother died before he graduated high school. As a result, Cornelius went to live with his older brother, who abused his wife.

It was Anna's freshmen year. Anna was excited to be away from home and free to talk to any guy she wanted to. When Anna lived at home, she knew Adeline would have never allowed her to date someone five years older than she was. Cornelius was a Vietnam-era veteran who had recently returned from military service. His college enrollment was during the same time as Anna's, and so was his course of study. Cornelius was on track to graduate from college at the same time as Anna. However, Anna graduated from college before Cornelius, and once she graduated, Cornelius did not attend any additional classes or graduate college. Anna did not know why Cornelius quit college, and Cornelius did not care to discuss why he stopped school with Anna.

As Anna recalled staring out of the dorm window at her future husband, she remembered Deanna asking, "Do you like him?" Anna did not respond but remembered thinking that Deanna was leaving later that year and Anna needed someone there with her. Cornelius did not live on campus but in a one-bedroom apartment off-campus. Anna found herself spending more and more time at Cornelius's apartment as they got to know one another.

Cornelius served in the military for approximately five years and received an honorable discharge; He always had an apartment filled with his army buddies. Anna would see them carrying large garbage bags filled with something, but she didn't ask any questions; she just remembered being happy to be away from home and being "grown." Later, Anna realized that her future husband and friends were carrying around large bags of marijuana they were smoking and selling. To this day, Anna doesn't care how many states legalize marijuana: she believes cannabis, alcohol, pills, and perhaps Cornelius's post-traumatic life experiences made him a paranoid schizophrenic, wife-beating maniac.

Midway through Anna's junior year of college, she and Cornelius got married. Five months after the marriage, the abuse started. Cornelius's abusive behavior came as a total surprise to Anna. Approximately one year later, Anna's college roommate, Bonita, who happened to be one of Anna's best friends, invited Anna and Cornelius to her wedding. On the day of her best friend's wedding, Anna was pleased with her best friend. She decided to wear the light blue, lace overlay dress, with a touch of white lace, to the wedding since this was the dress worn when she and Cornelius exchanged their wedding vows at a small gathering at Anna's mother's house. Anna recalled that she was fully dressed and remembered looking in the mirror, thinking about how much she loved her dress and how perfect it was for her to wear it to her best friend's wedding.

As Anna turned around from looking in the mirror, she was struck — wham! Anna's knees buckled under her body as she fell across the bed and onto the floor. Cornelius smashed Anna with a blow across her face that knocked her to the floor. Dazed and confused, Anna realized that all she could hear was, "Bitch, you think you look good, don't you?" Anna was stunned, and it took a minute for her to stand up. As she tried to gather her thoughts, she remembered seeing the lace torn from her dress and the dress ripped across the front. Anna recalled thinking, *I believe he hit me.* But, still, she wasn't quite sure because this was the first time that Cornelius hit Anna. Anna's eyes quickly scanned the room for an intruder; the blows to Anna's face and head caused some distortion in her thinking. So she looked up at Cornelius, holding what was left of the lace from her dress, with tears in her eyes, and asked, "Did you hit me?"

Cornelius immediately stretched out his hand as a gesture to help Anna to her feet and started apologizing, saying, "I am so sorry. I didn't mean to hit you, and you know how much I love you. I will never hit you again, I promise." Anna was devastated and heartbroken. Strangely enough, Anna found Cornelius's words not only comforting but also convincing.

At the wedding, Anna remembered that Bonita's grandmother had raised her. Bonita was the kindest soul you could ever meet, but Anna could not remember any of the details about her friend's wedding. She was sure she must have gone but could not remember any details. Anna was distraught about Cornelius hitting her.

Anna later learned that as a child, she used a blocking technique that helped her get past the traumatic events in her life and that some things were more challenging to block than others. Looking back, Anna recalled abusive and traumatizing incidents involving Cornelius in detail but had difficulty remembering certain other extreme events.

For example, although Anna was sure she had been hit several times after that, she could not recall the circumstances leading to when he abused her the second, third, fourth time, etc. She just knew she had been slapped, punched, kicked, cursed, on and on, and that her life, at the time, seemed like an eternal nightmare.

A few months after her friend got married, Anna became pregnant with her first child. She begged Cornelius to please not hit her while pregnant because it may harm the child and told him the authorities would know he was punching her. Cornelius must have believed her because he did not hit her during her pregnancy, but the mental anguish and abuse were nearly unbearable. After he could no longer beat her during the pregnancy, the name-calling started, and her new name became "Bitch." Cornelius would say things like:

"B_ _ _ _, you're never going to finish school."

"B _ _ _ _, why in the hell did you get pregnant in the first place? I never said I wanted a baby."

"B_ _ _ _, I don't want no baby."

"B_ _ _ _, I don't care if you are pregnant; you need to get a job."

"B_ _ _ _, I don't care if your ugly ass does try to leave; nobody else is going to want your ugly ass anyway."

"B_ _ _ _, why don't your lazy ass clean this house up?"

"B_ _ _ _, you can't cook; this food is nasty as hell."

"B_ _ _ _, who the hell are you talking to?"

"B_ _ _ _, who the hell are you looking at?"

As the months slowly dragged by, she was growing so tired of the name-calling and the criticisms. One day Anna was so hungry and just didn't feel like cooking at all. So she asked Cornelius to buy her something to eat. Cornelius bought Anna a Big Mac from McDonald's. While she was eating the Big Mac, Cornelius looked at her and said, "Bitch, your ass must have been starving to death." Anna responded to Cornelius and said, "See, you do care about me; that's why you bought me food." Cornelius looked at Anna and replied, "Bitch, what I did for you, I would do for any old dog."

Anna did not recall whether she told anyone about her abusive relationship because she was too ashamed. So, when she did happen to be around any family members or friends, or her husband's friends would visit, she would act as though everything was just fine. Anna stayed married to Cornelius for fourteen years, ten months, and twenty-two days. During that time, she had three children with him, and the acts of violence were too numerous to count. The beatings, kicking, cursing, punching, name-calling, etc., continued for what seemed to be a lifetime.

Anna left Cornelius three times before she finally left him for good. The first time Anna left, she went back home to her mother's house. However, Cornelius found her there and took the car so that Anna would not have transportation while at her mother's home. At the time, Anna's mother's brother from Virginia (Anna's Uncle Charlie) visited. When Anna went outside and found the car missing, Anna became frantic; at first, she thought perhaps a stranger had taken her car. Anna did not know it was Cornelius because it was nearly a two-hour drive from Anna's and Cornelius' home to her mother's house. Anna's uncle saw the person take the car early that morning, and he began to describe the person to Anna and her mother. Anna knew it was Cornelius from the description. Cornelius phoned Anna's mother shortly after that and told her, "I took the car from that Bitch, and it's nothing that you or that Bitch can do about it." "She is not getting the car back unless she comes home." When they were home, he would hide the keys or just remove car parts from the car so that the car would not start. The second time Anna left, she went to the Shelter for Battered Women. She stayed there thirty days (the maximum days allowed) and then went back home to Cornelius. Anna's mother was shocked and disappointed in Cornelius. When Anna first told her mother about Cornelius, her mother encouraged her to work things out. The following few times, Anna's mother said the Lord would work something out. After Anna's continued physical and mental abuse, Anna's mother encouraged her to leave Cornelius and feared for Anna's safety and that of her grandchildren.

Cornelius was a master manipulator. He had a home persona (abusive) and a public persona (perfect spouse), although the offensive home persona at home could spin around and become convincingly apologetic. In part, this is why Anna stayed married to Cornelius as long as she did. When Anna returned home from the shelter after the second time, a neighbor and one of Anna's few friends, Joelle and her husband Lionel, lived up the street. Joelle and Lionel were unable to have children of their own, so they adopted a child. While Anna was gone, Cornelius told Joelle that Anna said Joelle's adopted baby was ugly. Cornelius knew that Anna did not have many friends and that Joelle and Anna were good friends. Cornelius also knew that Joelle was sensitive about the adoption. Furthermore, Cornelius knew Anna would probably be coming back home, and this time he wanted to ensure Anna did not have anyone she could trust.

Sure enough, when Anna returned home and went up the street to speak to Joelle, Joelle met Anna at the back door. The first thing Joelle said was, "Why didn't you call me while you were gone?" The second thing Joelle said was, "Why in the hell did you say my baby was ugly?" Before Anna could speak, Joelle struck Anna and knocked her into a wooden railing on the porch. Again, Anna was stunned and couldn't believe what had just happened. Anna was fragile by this time. The tears were painful as they left her eyes, and she felt hopeless and too helpless to fight back. Just as Joelle raised her hand to strike Anna again, Joelle's husband, Lionel, grabbed her hand, picked her up, spun her around, and held her away from Anna. Anna left Joelle's house and went back home, where Cornelius was standing in the driveway. He immediately said to Anna, "See, I told you that bitch was not your friend, and you don't have any friends. All you got is me." Although In the past, Anna had confided in Joelle and Lionel about Cornelius' abusive patterns, Anna surmised that Cornelius must have convinced them that she was doing everything wrong. Cornelius always acted like the stand-up guy in front of other people but treated Anna harshly and was abusive behind closed doors.

The third time Anna left home, she had a semi-plan. Anna always believed that her mother, Adeline, had a strong intuition about things to come. Anna's mother told her when she went back home the second time that Cornelius would hit her two more times and that the second strike may be the one that kills her. Anna knew that Cornelius drank alcohol habitually, popped pills regularly, and smoked marijuana incessantly, but she did not know what else he may have been doing. Anna thought he might have been using drugs or having an extramarital affair. Anna searched for any explanation that would explain Cornelius' actions towards her.

Now, this third time of escape, it was a Friday night and storming heavily. Anna now had three small children with Cornelius. Anna could tell that Cornelius had either drank too much, popped too many pills, or not smoked enough of whatever because he was hell-bent on taking his anguish out on Anna and the children. Cornelius seemed drunk or high on drugs; he was cursing Anna, calling her ugly, cursing and calling the children ugly, threatening the children and Anna. Anna saw the bottle of whiskey sitting there, grabbed the bottle; she wanted to hit Cornelius with the bottle but instead decided to pour the Alcohol in the sink. Against her better judgment, Anna lost control, thinking that this may somehow get Cornelius' attention or he would not drink any additional alcohol that night. She made a terrible mistake, grabbing Cornelius's

Crown Royal© whiskey and beginning to pour it down the sink. As the sound went, "*gulp, gulp, gulp, gulp*," down the drain, Cornelius looked around with what seemed to be blood in his eyes. He became angry as Anna continued to pour out the whiskey. Cornelius rose to his feet and started toward Anna. He looked at Anna and declared, "Bitch, you have "f_ _ _ _ed" up now. I am going to put your bitch-ass through that wall." Anna's oldest child, who was eight years old, jumped between Anna and Cornelius, shouting, "Not today, Daddy—not today." Cornelius landed a blow across her son's face, leaving his handprints on the child's face. Barely missing the edge of the kitchen table, the child landed on the kitchen floor, hitting his head on the leg of one of the chairs at the table. Her son scrambled to his feet, went into the bedroom, and retrieved a small Phoenix Arms HP22A .22 Caliber Pistol. The child pointed the pistol at Cornelius. Anna was utterly shocked that the child knew where the gun was. Anna coaxed the weapon away from her son by telling him that she would shoot Cornelius herself. She said to her son, "let me do it, please, let me do it."

The police officer once told Anna that Cornelius must have known that in some cases, open-handed blows like a slap may be forgiven by the courts more readily as opposed to violent strikes with the fist. At this point, Anna knew she had no choice. It was now her life, the child's life, or the life of Cornelius. Anna's leaving had become inevitable. She had to save herself and her three children. Anna became despondent and regurgitated.

Anna had hidden a small bag that contained her identification, money, a name, and a phone number outside the house. Anna knew that the day of reckoning would come, and it was finally upon her. Before this day arrived, Anna sat her children down, showed them a hand gesture, and made them practice it a few times. She explained to them in no uncertain terms that if they saw her make this motion, it was time for them to run and follow her because she would be running too. That dreaded night, Anna used the hand motions. (*Using both hands, moving all fingers in a traveling motion-like her fingers were running, while counting to three, then clinching both fists, then suddenly tapping her fists together, crossing them at her chest*).

That stormy Friday night was like no other; it was an old-fashioned southern storm, threatening straight-line winds and full-blown tornadoes. The rain poured, the thunder roared, and the lightning flashed. Anna had no time to think about an umbrella, and there was no time to get a hat or any other protective clothing. Anna grabbed her youngest child, looked at the other two, gave the hand gesture, and took off out the door. By the time Anna snatched her hidden bag, the other two children were right on her heels. Anna never really knew how brave and intelligent her children were. They did not question their mother; they trusted her. Anna and her children walked, jogged, and ran to the nearest grocery store. Anna doesn't think any of them even had shoes on their feet. At the store, Anna took the number from the bag, tried desperately to hold back the tears, and covered the children with a blanket or cloth covering that a stranger had given her to shield them from the weather and to hide them from Cornelius; she dialed the domestic abuse hotline's number. The lady on the phone asked Anna to stay exactly where she was. Several minutes later, a police car arrived to pick up Anna and her three small children. The police officers took Anna to another parking lot, where Anna and her children were transferred to an unmarked car and were safely transported back to the shelter for battered women and children.

During the last time Anna stayed at the shelter, Anna made one friend, Sara. Sara was a Caucasian female, and Anna was African-American. However, they both seemed to have a special bond and connection. Anna and Sara both had small children, and they would talk each night about what appeared to be their shattered hopes and dreams for themselves and their children. Sara was at the shelter when Anna arrived, and Anna never thought to ask Sara how long she had been there. Anna left for work each day, while battered shelter staff provided care for Anna's children. All this time, Cornelius was aware of Anna's place of employment. Cornelius came to Anna's job more than once.

The last time he came to Anna's place of work, he accosted her in the hallway. Anna was walking with a co-worker. Cornelius grabbed Anna's arm, and Anna begged him to let her go. Anna's friend also begged Cornelius to release Anna's arm. Cornelius released Anna's arm, but not before severely striking Anna in the mouth. He hit Anna so hard, her nose and her lips bled. Anna and her co-worker hurriedly returned to Anna's office. The Office Director was standing in the doorway when they returned. The Director saw Anna's face and called campus security. She asked Anna what happened. Anna explained to her Director that she and her children were living in a battered families' shelter. Anna explained that her estranged husband had been stalking her, subsequently coming to her job and attacking her. Anna received treatment for her wounds, and the Director notified security that if Anna's estranged husband was ever seen on the hospital campus to have him arrested immediately.

On the day Cornelius attacked Anna at work, Anna returned to the refuge from work eager to talk to Sara and tell her what had happened. She found a note on her bed. The letter read, "Dear Anna, we had to leave; I left you some snacks for the kids. You made this living hell bearable for me, and I hope we meet again someday under better circumstances." The hottest and darkest tears ever poured down Anna's face. Anna knew she had lost Sara forever and missed her friend more than imaginable.

Days after Sara's departure, Anna and her children left the shelter. Thankfully, Anna and her children did not return to her home or Cornelius but lived in an affordable apartment complex. While there, Anna met Lorna, who showed her how to survive with three children and no other support. During this time, Anna had limited contact with her mother. Anna feared for her mother's safety, and she did not tell her that she was moving away from Cornelius. Anna knew of Cornelius' fury and how upset he would be after she left. Anna did not want him anywhere near her mother.

Leaving Cornelius was a stark realization for Anna because she now understood that she was alone with nothing to rely on but her faith. Lorna showed Anna how to shop for bargains at the store, how to clip and save coupons. But, most of all, Lorna showed Anna that being alone was not the worst thing that could have happened; and that aside from all else that was going on, Anna's first responsibility was to take care of herself, and then she could care better for her children. So Lorna showed Anna how to make her face up, how to keep her hair together, encouraged her to stay clean and neat at all times, and, most of all, encouraged Anna to keep the serenity prayer in her heart. Lorna was the kindest, most robust, most independent person that Anna had ever met.

Finally, Anna gathered enough strength and filed a court order. She divorced Cornelius and returned to her home, and kept her automobile. Despite a restraining order, Cornelius continued to harass Anna by not paying child support timely or showing up at the house, whether day or night, begging Anna to come in and promising her he would be better to her this time. Cornelius was to pay Anna child support each month for the children. He made it clear he would do absolutely nothing else to help Anna with the children. Because Cornelius was responsible for personally paying Anna, Cornelius would come to the house and wave a check toward Anna's face. Then he would pretend to hand Anna the check. When Anna would reach for the paper check, Cornelius would say, "Bitch, you need this, don't you?" Then he would drop the paper check on the ground and make Anna pick it up from the grass. This harassment and disrespect continued for quite some time.

One day, Anna had a male friend over when Cornelius brought the check. Cornelius immediately started to insult both Anna and her friend. Cornelius called Anna every name he could think of, including Cornelius' given expression to her of "bitch." When Cornelius finally left the premises, Anna's friend told her he could no longer visit her unless she filed a restraining order against Cornelius. Anna's friend was adamant that Cornelius's tirades would inevitably cause an unwanted outcome because the level of disrespect levied by Cornelius was intolerable. It was unacceptable for Anna, her friend, and the children. Anna dreaded and was reluctant to go back to court, fearing that Cornelius would stop paying the small amount of child support each month for the children. It took several court appearances to finalize the restraining order and ensure direct deposits of child support payments from Cornelius's paycheck instead of having Cornelius pay her directly. The court-issued restraining order did not matter to Cornelius. Cornelius continued to break into Anna's house. Frequently, Cornelius would place dead rodents or other animal parts in Anna's bed so that when she turned back the covers, she would discover the mutilated animal parts or rodents. Finally, Anna had security bars installed on all the windows and doors.

Glory be to God, one beautiful day, and many years later, the harassment ended; and life had a sense of normalcy for Anna again. By no means was Anna's life easy after divorcing Cornelius. Anna recalled moments when she considered suicide. During one of her darkest hours, she fell asleep and had a dream that appeared as a vision, as though she talked to *Jesus* (or her peace angel). Jesus is the *religious leader, revered in Christianity, and regarded by most Christians as God's incarnation*. Anna recalled vividly seeing a figure standing among the brightest light she had ever seen. She said the figure, whom she believed to be Jesus had arms that reached toward her. At Jesus's feet was a large container similar to a large round tub or round basket. Jesus spoke to her and said, "I want you to put all your troubles and worries into this basket. Then, let Me carry your load for a while."

Anna recalled that somehow she put all her worries in the basket: the food she needed for the children, clothing, money for school supplies, utilities, house payments, gasoline for the car, car note, etc. Anna recalled thinking as fast as possible because she wanted to get all the primary necessities into the basket. She desperately needed help and felt sure that this lighted figure she believed to be Jesus would indeed carry her burdens if she could get them into the basket fast enough. When Anna was sure nearly everything was in the basket, the figure in the light proceeded to take up the basket. Immediately, Anna shouted, "Wait, I forgot something."

Standing in a light brighter than the sun, Jesus said, "No, you cannot put all your troubles in this basket. Surely, it would be best if you carried some of them for yourself. Otherwise, you may as well have committed suicide when you considered it." In her dream, an angel is standing near Jesus. Anna began to cry what the angel termed as "dark tears." At once, the angel said. "Go now, and remember weeping lasts for a night, but joy cometh in the morning." Jesus immediately wiped the dark tears from Anna's eyes and told her, "For your tears are no longer dark, but filled with light." Anna did not know it at the time, but weeping lasts for a night, but joy cometh in the morning was a part of Verse 5, Psalm 30. A song for the dedication of the temple of David. The entire Psalm, as written by the New International Version of the Bible, reads as follows:

A psalm. A song. For the dedication of the temple of David.

Psalm 30 New International Version

I will exalt you, LORD,
for you lifted me out of the depths
and did not let my enemies gloat over me.
2 LORD my God, I called to you for help,
and you healed me.
3 You, LORD, brought me up from the realm of the dead;
you spared me from going down to the pit.

4 Sing the praises of the LORD, you his faithful people;
praise his holy name.
5 For his anger lasts only a moment,

but his favor lasts a lifetime;
weeping may stay for the night,
but rejoicing comes in the morning.

6 When I felt secure, I said,
"I will never be shaken."
7 LORD, when you favored me,
you made my royal mountain stand firm;
but when you hid your face,
I was dismayed.

8 To you, LORD, I called;
to the Lord I cried for mercy:
9 "What is gained if I am silenced,
if I go down to the pit?
Will the dust praise you?
Will it proclaim your faithfulness?
10 Hear, LORD, and be merciful to me;
LORD, be my help."

11 You turned my wailing into dancing;
you removed my sackcloth and clothed me with joy,
12 that my heart may sing your praises and not be silent.
LORD my God, I will praise you forever.

When Anna woke from her dream or vision, her face was wet with tears, and the sunlight streamed through the window with piercing light, a light brighter than she had ever known. Anna believed that it took Jesus, the incarnation of God Himself, to sustain her throughout her life experiences.

When Anna arose the next day, she knew and accepted that her Creator existed as an inner-spirit and higher power, which created a sense of peace in her life. She was allowed to continue her journey through her faith-based relationship with her spiritual protectors and the serenity prayer, written by Reinhold Niebuhr.

CHAPTER SEVEN

"CREEPING COMPROMISES"

GRACE:

I grew up in a home where abuse frequently occurred. Growing up, my father was an alcoholic. My mother and father were always fighting. We had bills, and, at times, the utility companies turned off our utilities. Not having utilities meant we did not have electricity, heat, or water. As an adult, the childhood struggles made me withdrawn or self-conscious. I think adult abuse victims go through abusive relationships and make excuses for their marriages. Living in a home, in marriage, and finding out that my husband was gay, and finding out that he was using marijuana every day, was nearly unbearable. I suffered from mental abuse, cursing, and name-calling, as he was doing many little things. He was also lying and talking about me and telling lies to my friends and church members. He would lie about how many friends I had or did not have and about seeing other men or having affairs. He lied when he said he would never strike a woman. Primarily he lied about what he did and where he went.

I do not want to say what year we were married, but I lived with him for one year and was engaged to him for one year, and after then, I left. I never did marry again. I stayed for a year, maybe a year and a half, and I didn't marry anymore after then. He died from unknown causes a few years after I left him. I went through many changes with him: He would curse me out in the street, he would come home in a bad mood, and he would curse us and run the children and me out into the road. I don't know how I survived, but I know I did not handle it very well. I finally decided I just couldn't stay there any longer after he told me that he intended to kill me, then himself.

When we were riding in the car one time, I told him that I felt like I needed to leave. He had asked me to go for a ride so we could talk. I got my baby and got into the car. When I got into the car, he headed straight to the bridge and said he would drive the car off the bridge. He threatened to kill us and leave my baby by the side of the road or somewhere else to raise the baby or do something worse. I started crying, hollering, and screaming. Then, I started praying; something told me just to hush and pray. After much prayer, many tears, screams, begging, and pleading, he decided to drive the car back home. After that, I made up my mind; that near-death experience was the last straw. The first chance I got, without him knowing, I packed enough stuff for the baby. I left and got my brothers to go back and get some of my other things.

Without the Holy Spirit in me, I do not believe I would have survived. I know some may not agree or believe this, but the Holy Spirit would talk to me the whole time. It would tell me things, but I wouldn't listen to the voice of God. I just refused to believe that it was telling me the right thing. You know, when the Holy Spirit speaks to us in that tiny, small voice, we need to listen. But I just would not listen.

I may have somewhat recovered, but I still have not fully recovered. I know for the longest while, my hair would not grow. I believe it was because of the stress I had endured. Finally, my hair started to grow back, and I felt like the healing process from all the abuse had begun. When it started growing, I thought, *I must heal and get over some of the trauma.*

I would try to talk to my friends about what I was going through, but they didn't want to listen or hear about being abused. The people at church were always on his side and did not want to listen to it. I could talk to my mother; she was the only person who would listen. Then, after he died, years later, some of them wanted to talk about how sorry they were about what I had to go through. Really? Before, when I tried talking to the people at church or explaining what was happening to me, they would say, "Awe, don't tell your business." Or, "People at the church are already talking about you, and they believe it is you, not him"; or, "He's so lovely, so, why don't you just try to bear with it and don't say anything else about it?" No one at that church wanted to listen to me.

I wanted to find a way to make things better, and I often look back, trying to figure out what could have made my situation better. The only thing I could come up with is that I should have listened to the Holy Spirit and prayed more, listened to the Word of the Lord, and not gotten caught up in what all the people at the church were saying. Most of all, I should have avoided the whole thing by not getting involved with that man in the first place. I was in a hurry to be married to someone. I should have been patient and waited on the Lord to send me the right person. The signs that he was not suitable for me were there; he was giving off signals. Because you see, warnings are always given by men or humankind when something is not correct; it's just that a lot of times, people ignore them. I did not pay close enough attention, and I am thinking that way about my problem. I should have listened and paid more immediate attention than being in a hurry to get with someone.

I should have known he was gay, or bi-sexual, or something. He showed what I thought were gay tendencies. I saw the signs, and I ignored them. I now know he was having sex with both men and women when I was married to him. Yes, men and women, men and women. One time, he got into trouble with a young boy at a school. He lost his job, and they put him in jail for some young boy. He denied the charges, and he was able to get out of jail but had lost his job. After that, he started to come home later and later or not at all. He worked at a hotel and often talked about another man who was a minister. He would say that the minister was a prostitute on the side, had a wife, and preached every Sunday. I knew he was watching the man in my heart, and he either wanted to do what the man was doing or be with the man. But, I didn't listen to that small, inner voice. And, sure enough, he got to where he didn't want to come home from work at all.

One night, he didn't come home, and something told me he was telling me a lie about why. He told me he had to help his friend who owned a store. There were many different lies. He was not at the store; he was with a man at the hotel. Once I found this out, other men started coming forward and telling me he had made passes at them and that he had been doing this quite often for some time. Before he told me this, he was so angry. I thought he might kill me at the hotel. Internally and externally, I was distraught. I could not believe this was happening to me; it was a "rude awakening," a "reality check," a "breakthrough," or something. I don't know what to call it. I mean, the man was all but a professional gospel singer. I am telling you, the man could sing classical gospel musicals like Wintley Phipps and those Three Tenors. He could sing like them; he had a beautiful voice.

I would tell anyone who is in an abusive relationship not to waste any more time in it. Find a way to get out. An abusive relationship is not worth it. Life is important. Love yourself more and watch out for the little things that happen early on in the relationship. Watch out for those minor, subtle warning signs. When you start dating, dating someone long enough to find out more about that person, especially before you marry them.

Don't be afraid to pray and ask the Lord for guidance, and if and when He gives you a warning, pay attention to it. Find out about a person—somebody always knows, and they will tell you. Check around, find out everything you can about the person you want to date. It will be worth it. I know women who did not live long enough to get out of their bad relationships.

I know one lady that was married to a gay man, and when she found out, she confronted him – and she went to leave, and he killed her. Yeah, people don't always get out of their abusive situations. So, I repeat this, find out everything you can about potential dates. If you find yourself in an abusive relationship, take precautions. Some people say they have changed—sometimes they do, but—give it time, that's what I mean. I wouldn't rush; don't rush into a relationship.

If you come from a home where violence was prevalent, pay even closer attention to your relationships. I believe that domestic violence follows a pattern; it's like a trail or a curse that goes on and on, and you have to break that curse or habit.

In closing, I would like to re-emphasize, always pray and ask the Lord to guide you in developing your relationships. Try to find out as much as you can about the other person and take your time. Most of all, watch out for the little things—they call the "*creeping compromise*." Those are the little things that mean a lot. They seem small, but they are critical. I've seen people that got these little, bitty sins, little, bitty things that we don't watch, and then the small things that he does. And, you think, oh, that's nothing when it's something big. As I say, I thought he might be gay, and I ignored that. No, I might change him. Little, bitty things, as I say—they say the devil comes in like a stranger in the night—sin— and he creeps in, little by little because there are some things you do not want to handle. He might grab, pull, or shake you something. Any snatching, grasping, or holding actions were uncomfortable and showed his extreme jealousy. The tiny things we look over before getting deeply involved in a relationship need addressing, and they need a resolution.

The devil does his work one tiny step at a time. At least, that is what I have always heard.

CHAPTER EIGHT

"OLE DUMB STUFF" "LORD, ONE OF US IS GOING TO DIE."

EMMA:

The first indication that I was in an abusive relationship or environment was when a man hit me. I can't give you an exact date, but I can tell you that years ago when I was in a relationship with my second child's father, it became abusive. At the time, I did not know that he was on drugs; I just thought he was a drinker. I didn't think he was doing illegal drugs. And, he was always accusing me of flirting. You know, like if someone said something to me, or if I would laugh back at them, he would take that as though I was flirting or whatever. So, this one particular night, even though I was pregnant with my daughter at the time, we got into this argument. So, when we got into this argument, he pinned me in a corner–one of the corners in our home—because we lived together. So he pinned me in the corner of a room. I think it was the dining room at the time. He had me cornered. I couldn't get out; I couldn't move to the left; I couldn't move to the right. He pinned me, and somehow, I was able to break loose and get away from him. I ran to the kitchen and grabbed a knife.

I was so out of my mind, you know. I just started swinging. And, I could hear myself cursing and saying, "Come on, come on, hit me now, and hit me now." You know, I was swinging the knife in a blind rage, and the next thing that I knew, he had left. About three or four hours later, he came back with the police. And so, it was raining that night, I will never forget it, and before the policeman came, my dad asked me, "Did you cut that boy?" I was like, "No, Daddy, I ain't cut him," and he was like, "Are you sure?"

"Yeah," I said, "He shouldn't have touched me. I got the knife, but I never used the knife or anything." He said, "Well, I saw blood on the porch. Are you sure?" I said, "I'm sure." After that, he came back with the policemen, and sure enough, I had cut him; he had three or four stitches. So, the policeman told me that anytime there is a knife incident like this one, they had to investigate it. And so, he had said to them that I had stabbed him, so they came to the house. But that was the first time and pretty much the only time he was physically abusive toward me. You know, he hit me with his hands. No other man has ever put his hands on me. You see, I suffered emotional abuse, but that was the only time a man had put his hands on me and hit me.

Hitting me did not end the relationship, and I didn't even know that I was pregnant at the time. I, later on, found out that I was pregnant with my daughter. I endured the whole time because when I got pregnant with my daughter, he and I weren't even married. And so, when I got to be about seven months pregnant, he and I got married because I told him I did not want to bring my baby into the world without being married. So we wound up getting married, and I would say probably about my eighth month, or somewhere around that time frame, he did some "ole dumb stuff." Ahh, he called me because he was working and told me to check on him because he felt terrible. I asked him what was going on, and he said to me that he was on his way and would be home shortly. Well, it soon turned into the following day. So, remind you, we had one car, so he never did come home.

He came home the next day, like early morning, I'm talking like nine or ten, or whatever. So, I was so mad at him, so angry. I had taken so much abuse from this man throughout our relationship. I was sitting there, just waiting. I had told myself before he came, I said, "Lord, one of us is going to die. You know I'm tired of this. You know I'm just tired. One of us is not going to make it through this whenever I see him." So, when he came home, he told me he was on his way home. He called that morning; I guess he wanted to see what kind of mindset I had, how I was talking. But, I was pleasant, really nice because I wanted him to call. When he called, he told me he was on his way home. When he came home, I went into the kitchen and boiled some water. And, when he came home, I said, "Where have you been all night? I told you I wasn't feeling good, and I told you I was hurting, and you told me you were on your way home." He said, "Yeah, I did." And, that rage set in, I went in the kitchen, got that pot of water, and I "threw it on his ass."

Now mind you, when that water hit him, from his head to his whatever, I saw a look in his eyes that I had never seen in a person's eyes before, and I just knew, at that moment, I was dead, because I have never seen a look like that in nobody's eyes. But, before he attacked me, he took the lamp, and he hit my birdcage. He broke the light and broke the birdcage. I guess if he had not grabbed the birdcage and the lamp before he grabbed me, I would not be here today. But I think he took most of his anger out by hitting the birdcage with the light. Hitting those things calmed him down some. But then, after that, he grabbed me like in a chokehold. Now I'm eight months pregnant, and he grabbed me from behind with his arms around my neck. So, I fell on the floor, which I had carpet on the floor. So, he's choking me, and I'm trying to get away, you know, all this pressure on me, on my knees. So I wound up getting rug burns on both my knees and at some point, he just let me go. But I thought for sure he was going to kill me right then and there because he had his arms around my neck. Very abusive, very, very vicious.

I stayed in that relationship with him until my daughter turned about three. That's when I finally said it's enough because I just could no longer take this "ole dumb stuff" anymore.

I stayed that long because I think it was right after my daughter was born, he decided to get himself together. I was already going to church, so he started going to church. Ah, we got in the choir, you know, so things were getting better, you know, and ah, I guess whatever demons he was fighting, it was better because now, he was going to church, you know, whatever. But, what ended it? I will never forget what ended it. I had this close girlfriend that I had gone to high school with, and we were together during church. We get a watch night meet at church, where we stayed on New Year's Eve, where we prayed until the new day. He was sitting to my left, and she was sitting to my right. So I hurried over toward her because I was trying to see the minister bringing the Word, you know, I couldn't see him. You know, I couldn't see his face from where I was sitting, so I just moved over.

So beginning sometime New Year's day, you know, like after church, he starts saying stuff to me like, "So what?--The two of you all gay?" There was no plausible explanation for this statement. He had always falsely accused me of affairs with anyone I became friends with, whether male or female. I said, "What, boy, it's a brand new day; what are you talking about?" The fights continued for a while. After that, I gave up. He changed my outlook on relationships, and his abusive actions have caused me to avoid developing sound relationships to this day. My advice to anyone in an abusive relationship is to get out before it gets worse.

CHAPTER NINE

BACKSTABBING

CORONA:

My first indication that I was in an abusive situation or environment was when I realized I was suffering physically and mentally. It started probably like six months after I started dating this guy I had known for years. We started dating, and I was a single parent of one, and he was helping me raise my child. One day I didn't come to the door fast enough. Well, I was living with my mom; he had his place in Tuskegee, Alabama. He knocked on my mom's entry, and I didn't make it to the door fast enough. When I opened the door, he hit me. Unfortunately, I had no idea he was abusive before the first time he hit me when I opened that door. After that, I cannot tell you how many times he hit me. The abuse lasted for more than eight years. Then, after about eight years, our daughters said that they couldn't take it anymore.

I can't say exactly why I stayed with him all those years. I kind of fell in love with the beautiful things he would do. And, after all the physical abuse, he would always come behind it with impressive ideas. But, when I knew it was too much was when he was still cheating. And, this person, I did marry that person, but he was always hustling. And when I realized that, it was just too much. One night when I was at home, I questioned him about the cheating, so he jumped on me in the yard, and we got in the car. Well, he forced me into the car that night. And, he went down the road going 95 mph, down Martin Luther King

Highway in Tuskegee, Alabama. And, when we got down the highway, it had been an accident on the road. So he turned around and started coming back toward my house, driving fast (*Corona's voice breaking - struggling to continue*). The entire time we were riding, I was holding onto the Bible, praying. So, when we got down Pleasant Springs Drive, it was either we hit the bus or the trees. So, into the trees, we went. We flipped over like four times. When I got out of the car, my face and eyes were black from bruises. I don't know whether it happened before the accident or afterward, but I did hit my face, and I know I blanked out. So, I was like, "I blanked out."

On my side of the car, there wasn't a dent. But, his side of the car had crushed over to my side of the vehicle, and, um, I stayed in the car for a second. I kept calling his name, calling his name. And, I thought maybe, I thought perhaps he had died. The car was smoking, so I got out of the vehicle, and a car was coming down the road. It's funny how it worked out; the same person that saved me in the street—because I couldn't see—was the same person that had broken into my car (*chuckle*) a week or two earlier. So, they took me to the house, and they went back to him. So, he was awake by the time they got back. So they took me to the house, and they went and picked him up. And, my dad took us to the emergency room, where we had to have MRIs and all of that. But, right then, I knew that it wasn't—that was a lot, and I also thought that maybe he did this because he lost his mom and dad.

So, after that, and I said that was enough then, but after that, he took me to his mom's grave and proposed to me, and I married him. Big mistake, big mistake. After I married him, I questioned him again. But he didn't do anything at that time; he waited until he came home. While I was home asleep, he stabbed me. I ran to get away from him. I ran to some apartments, and my cousins came to the apartment, picked me up, and took me to the hospital, where I had to have several stitches. After that, I talked to my daughters. They said, "Mom, look at what has happened, and all you do is fuss and fight." One of my daughters, which is my oldest daughter, I asked her. I was like, "Do you want Mommy and Daddy to break up?" Which is not her dad, but that's the only dad she knew. And she was like, "Yes because all you do is fight all the time." But, for my other daughter, it was hard for her to accept that because that was her father. So, it was hard for her, and she went through a lot because of our break-up, but she finally got better. My daughters were between seven and ten years old at the time, and I knew I needed to do something.

I stayed with him for nearly eight years. I am not sure how I survived all the years of torment. I would pray, and I would always try to do everything the way he liked it. And I never went anywhere. Other than that, I just worked or tried to sleep the pain away. I would take sleeping pills and just try to sleep the pain away. I would talk to my family and occasionally speak with friends, but I didn't tell them about what was going on in my personal life. I am sure they knew something. I tried to hide my feelings or emotions but what I could not hide were the physical scars. Some scars they could see; many abrasions they could not see. I never told them how often this happened. I prayed; I prayed a lot. I prayed that things would change, but they never did.

I do not feel I will ever recover from the abuse that I suffered. Because now, when I meet a person, and he tries to love me, I mistreat him. I don't know how to treat a guy because of all the things that have happened to me. I never sought professional help. I am not sure what I could have done to make the situation different or better, but I believe I should have gotten out of the relationship the first time he hit me. I would tell a younger person or anyone in an abusive relationship to get out in the beginning because no one deserves to be beaten or mistreated. Just leave when you first see the signs that it's coming. If you do not go, you may not make it out.

I knew it was time to go after the stabbing and the car accident. And, I forgot about the gun incident. I don't know if the gun was loaded or not. I was sitting on my front porch, and he came and said, if I want to leave, then go. And he had a gun to my head, clicking it; I don't know if it was something in the chamber or what, but all I know is that it was terrifying. I think that was scarier than the car or the stabbing. I just sat there. I was scared, wondering if the next pull of the trigger was it. I asked myself if I was going to die that night or not. I thought about how his mother had been killed from domestic abuse. His auntie and her boyfriend still fought, and his mom tried to break them up, and the (auntie's) boyfriend stabbed his mother in the back and killed her, trying to get to the auntie. And he (my husband) had to be raised by that same auntie, which still stuck around with the (*backstabbing*) boyfriend that killed his mother. His mother died from a stabbing, and he stabbed me more than once. He stabbed me like five times (*Corona counting and showing stab wounds).*

All I can say, and I can't say this enough time, is what I said before: When you see the first signs of abuse, leave. Even if it is only a push, leave; go because that is how it starts. It starts with more minor things. I am not sure about the traits or signs of an abuser and how a person can tell if their partner might abuse them. I believe it is different for every person. For some people, it may be like one minute the person is happy and another, the person turns into another person that yells and all of that. I watched all of that, but since my husband and I are no longer together, I haven't gotten into a relationship where someone stays with me for more extended periods. I cannot sleep around a man because of trust issues as a result of my abusive ex-husband.

CHAPTER TEN

"DARKEST NIGHT OF THE SOUL"

ALLISON:

I am from Belzoni, Mississippi, in the Delta. And I started dating Percy, who had moved from Chicago to Belzoni. At the beginning of the relationship, we got into an altercation a couple of months after I was with him. And, I think he was trying to jump on me or something. My mom was living with me at that time, and we made him leave the house. I ended up calling the police because he put holes in all four of my tires and made them flat. And then another time we were dating, my current twenty-three-year-old was a baby, and we moved to Chicago and lived with his mother. His mother told us we could not live in her house unless we were married. Not having anyplace else to go, we ended up getting married in Chicago. It had been two months, and I wouldn't say I liked Chicago.

Therefore, I moved back to Belzoni, Mississippi. Approximately one week after we moved back to Belzoni, he stayed at the hotel all night with another woman. When I went to the hotel and caught him with the other woman, he jumped on me, striking me, until he had given me a black eye. Because he constantly cheated, we separated. After the separation, he would follow me around. Whenever I attempted to leave home or go out on a date, he would follow me around. He would chase me from one street to another; it did not matter. One night, he finally caught up with me.

Although we had a legal separation, he questioned me profusely, asking, "Where do you think you are going?" After I said, "It is not your business," he got into my car, with me still in the driver's seat. I decided to drive around the corner to a friend's house to call the police safely. I got out of the car, and he jumped out of the vehicle. I told him again, "I don't know why you are following me; you and I are not together." And, immediately, he began beating me so bad. He kicked me and kept on kicking me until my eyes were blue, black, and purple. I could not see anything. I could not even see my child; he severely injured my face. My face was swollen, bruised, and my skin moved like gelatin; it was so swollen. My little boy was only four and a half, and my little girl was just an arm baby. So, I left my home in Belzoni, and I moved to Jackson, Mississippi. I was doing my best, my best, to try and leave the abusive and violent situation. I had stayed in the relationship through a lot when he first made my tires flat, giving me the black eye and all the rest of the beatings. But, this time was different. I had my two children, and I had to "run away."

Shortly after I moved to Jackson, his mother moved from Chicago to Jackson. And, guess what? You guessed it. I was stupid enough to go back to him again. Shortly after I went back to him, he would take my car, ride all the gas out, and would bring it back to me on empty. Finally, one day he just took my car. I worked for the post office in Jackson; I could not get to work after taking my car. After he took my car, I needed him to pick me up and take me to work. He told me he had not come home because he did not have my car, and the police found my car somewhere, and that someone had taken a gun and shot bullet holes throughout my vehicle. Honestly, I believed he had taken a gun and shot my car up himself. The insurance paid me for the car, but I am pretty sure if he did not do it, he had someone else do it to be dirty and mean to me so that I would be afraid of him.

After everything that had happened, I would put gas in my car after getting the car back. He would still take the car and drive it around until it was empty. Once again, he came to pick me up for work, and he was late. I asked him why he was picking me up for work late. He became so angry, he forced my head against the glass car window and bruised my face, and once more gave me a black eye. He said, "Bitch, I am going to kill you tonight." I left home and went to live with my brother. I knew, if I wanted to live, I had to do something. Because of the various police reports concerning Percy's violent behavior toward me, Percy stayed on the run from the police for several weeks. Finally, the police arrested him.

On and off, I honestly cannot remember how long we were together. Through it all, we got married, and Percy beat me too many times to count. Yet, I stayed. I have questioned myself over and over as to why I stayed. I prayed every day that one day I would be able to walk away from Percy, and eventually, I was able to leave him.

Once I left Percy and separated for quite some time, I began dating Jackson. Percy threatened to harm Jackson, so I divorced Percy. Jackson was good to me for the first two years, but, like Percy, dating Jackson turned out to be a mistake as well. I was tormented by Jackson mentally and emotionally for nearly fourteen years. Jackson would put the children and me out of our home. When he would put us out, it was humiliating and indescribable. We would have to leave home and stay with friends or a hotel. We were living with Jackson, but I went out and bought my own house.

Even though I had my own house, the children and I continued living with Jackson. I would leave him, stay gone about a month, and then go back. Soon, I started to catch him with different women over and over. Then, he was diagnosed with prostate cancer. I was there for him; I helped take care of him. Finally, we were at his mother's house, and he was acting funny to me; I didn't know why. I always knew that he cheated on me with different women multiple times. But, what I did not know was that he would leave me for one of them. In September, he locked my son and me out of the house and changed the locks on the doors. Thank God I had bought my own house, and Devon, my son, and I had someplace to go. Once he put us out, he moved a woman into our home immediately. The woman he moved into our house had seven children. We had been together for thirteen years and four months. Most of those years, he told me, "I was the love of his life," and that he had met his "soulmate." So, for me, I felt like I just couldn't figure it out. I couldn't figure out why he did not want me or why he didn't love me. I was there for him. I tried to do everything a wife is supposed to do. I didn't cheat; I did everything I knew a wife was supposed to do for a husband. At this point, I was questioning myself as to why. What did I do wrong? Why does he want her? Why doesn't he want me? I starting researching and reading stuff; I was desperately looking for an answer because my self-esteem was so low.

I mean, my self-esteem was literally at "ground zero." What I learned was that I did not love myself. I loved him more than I had ever loved myself. I went through the darkest days of my life. I cried every single day. I would do my best to take care of Devon and go to work, but I cried every day. I did not understand. Why did I have to go through this? Why did I allow myself to go through this for so long? Even though I stayed with him for thirteen, almost fourteen years, why? I know the first two years were good, but why? The other years were pure hell. But, I could not figure out why I could not leave this man. I am telling you, it made me very suicidal. I wanted to commit suicide because I felt like my life was unbearable without this man. I could not and did not want to live without this man; I could not deal with that. He was with another woman, and I had to cut all ties with him. I deleted his number from my phone. I did not talk to him. It did not matter; I was at the point whey I never wanted to fall in love again. I never wanted another man, and I just wanted this man. Currently, I am single, and my focus is trying to make enough money to support Devon and me.

He now takes care of the woman with the seven children. She doesn't work because he told her she did not have to work. He is now married to her, taking care of her children, but he will not do anything for Devon. I have learned a hard lesson, and the journey was painful. But, I have had to understand my self-worth. I want to be loved and respected because I cannot go through this physical, mental, and emotional pain anymore; I just can't.

I later learned that Jackson cheated on me for ten or eleven of the thirteen years and four months we were together. During those years, I would ask Jackson if there was another woman, and he would deny it. Jackson was bringing the women to our home. At times, there would be three different women calling Jackson's phone. I finally met one of the ladies he was dating for three years while he was dating me. The woman told me she was in love with Jackson and that she was the love of his life and his soulmate. When I asked Jackson about her specifically, he told me he had been involved with her but had ended their relationship. I have been through so much now until I had no desire to date anyone at all.

After three years had passed and I had been away from Jackson, I met an older man named Mr. Anthony. Mr. Anthony was fifteen years older than me, and he and his wife were separated. Mr. Anthony and I talked as friends for two or three months before we started dating. One day, I called Mr. Anthony's phone, and he did not answer. So, I went by his house to check on him. And, there she was, one of Jackson's women coming out of Mr. Anthony's house. I could not believe it. So, I stopped talking to Mr. Anthony. Mr. Anthony called me often, but I just could not bring myself to begin dating him again. Well, my birthday came, and he called on my birthday. Mr. Anthony was a smooth talker. He would send flowers to my job, call constantly, and leave sweet voicemail messages; most messages would be apologetic, advising me that I had misunderstood what I saw. He was showing up at my house, knocking on my door, and coming to my job. I finally told him I was seeing someone else. I wanted to persuade him to stop contacting me. When I did like him, he did not wish to have me. Then and now, I do not have the patience for-- I'm sorry, the bull shit. I just do not have it. I have been through so much; I don't even know if I'll ever have the tolerance of a relationship. The abuse that I have suffered has messed me up so badly that I go to work and come home.

Why I keep choosing these abusive, emotionally draining men, I do not know. I don't know if a person sends out negative vibes and attracts this type of garbage into their life. My self-esteem was so low. And guess what, I drew the same kind of garbage over and over in my life. Mr. Anthony was a nice, good-looking older man. When I met him, it felt like I had met my soulmate, the love of my life. I was thinking; *Now this is a well-rounded man, a church-going man, a God-fearing man.* For me, his actions were just unbelievable. I thought to myself, *Oh, my God, what is wrong with me that I keep attracting this same type of garbage into my life?* I told my cousin from Texas that I love him, but I just know he's not the right one for me. I could just tell he was not the right one. So, right now, I just do not have time for anybody.

You ask, what I could have done differently, or what I could do differently to meet a better type of man. I don't know because I think I am a great woman. I am a dependable woman, a God-fearing woman, and, I mean, I go to work, I don't cheat. But, I still wonder why I attract this same type of guy into my life, I don't know. I haven't talked to anyone professionally. But I have never gotten over Percy, Devon's father. I haven't spoken to anyone because I believe the first thing they or anybody might say is that you are crazy or need medication. And, I would say, "No, I am not crazy." A man abused me for so many years. And, I don't know if I am ever going to be ready to date again.

I have gone through the "darkest night of the soul." Right now, I am on a spiritual journey. I feel like God is trying to tell me that I need to get motivated – to teach other women about having low self-esteem so intense that they allow men to abuse them as I did. Maybe this way, they will not go through what I have gone through. I went through a rough time when I was suicidal and did not want to live. And suicide is so natural for me because my best friend killed himself. He was there for me. But, I regret that my emotional state from all the physical turmoil and trauma that I suffered did not allow me to be there for him.

I would tell anyone, woman, girl, or whomever, if you are in an abusive relationship, please walk away. Walk away, do not continue to stay. My first abusive relationship with Percy was physically harmful, as well as emotionally and mentally traumatizing. It was more physical abuse, and I was able to walk away. But, I could never figure out why I could not walk away from my emotionally and mentally draining relationship with Devon's father.

I was a woman with three children with three different daddies. I suppose that having three children with three other fathers was part of why I wanted to stay with Jackson. My oldest child's father (Xavier) left me. He did not wish to have me. Then I met my husband (Percy), an abusive cheater, and I had to leave him to save my life. Then Jackson knew what I had gone through, and he turned around and did the same thing; cheating on me with multiple women. I stayed with Jackson because of Devon. I was single and working in the public school system, not making enough money. I was afraid; afraid that I would not have enough money and I won't be able to do the things to create a comfortable life for my family and myself.

Jackson had put Devon's brother (Timothy) out of the house while still in school. Yet, I stayed with him. Jackson said that his mother had put him out of the house at seventeen years of age, and Timothy had turned seventeen, so it was time for him to get out. Therefore, Timothy moved down the street with another guy. Shortly after that, at the age of seventeen, someone shot Timothy in the head; miraculously, he survived. That is when I bought the house. My cousin from Chicago helped me buy the house, and I paid my cousin. So, yeah, I stayed with Jackson, in part, because of Devon.

I always prayed and asked God to give me the strength to walk away from Jackson. I even went to a psychic, the lady who reads cards, because I thought maybe he had put something on me, something like voodoo. Because I could never walk away from him, I just did not know what to think. I could not walk away from this relationship. Even when I left, I would only stay gone for about one month and then go back. As I said earlier, finally, Jackson left me for another woman. Jackson had the woman at what was then the home we shared. I went there and knocked on the door. Jackson came outside and told me that his woman was there and that she had spent the night. I know I keep saying some of this repeatedly, but I just can't get over how he put me out of our home and moved another woman in there. I didn't talk to him after that until a month later. When I did speak with him, he said, "It has nothing to do with anything that you did; it's all on me." I told him, "Well, if I died, right now, today, I know that I did what I had to do for you. I did not leave you; you left me."

He took pictures and put them on Facebook of him and her together. Jackson was an entertainer. He was a blues singer, and I knew by the clothes he had on and the gold teeth in his mouth that he was with her when he was with me. So, he started dating the woman and moved the woman in. The woman stopped working six months after they got together. She had not worked and recently got a job approximately one month ago. But, he would take care of her and her seven kids. According to him, none of those children were his children because he had prostate cancer. He had surgery, and after the surgery, the doctors told him he would never be able to have sex again. Jackson has to wear pull-ups or a diaper because he has leakage from the surgery.

Jackson proposed to Sharon (the other woman with the seven children) at a gig during one of his performances. In response to Jackson's proposal, Sharon told Jackson about an invitation to a black-and-white party at a friend's house. Jackson's mother (Clarice) also received an invitation to the party. When Clarice arrived at the party, there were quite a few people there, all of them dressed in black and white. The minister was also there. Clarice asked Sharon what was going on. Sharon told Clarice, "Oh, top this." All the people were there for Sharon's and Jackson's wedding ceremonies. Jackson had no idea that it was his wedding day.

To me, mental and emotional abuse was just as bad, if not worse, than the physical abuse I suffered because the physical wounds healed, but the trauma from the mental and emotional abuse just seem never to leave. I can't and have never really recovered.

Three years had passed and gone since Jackson put us out. I haven't communicated with him. But, as a father, his name is still on the contact list at my son's school. Devon asked Jackson why he put us out of our home. Approximately six months later, Jackson told Devon that I stopped communicating with him. He told Devon that if he wanted to see him, he should act up at school and then ask the school to call his father, not his mother. So, that is what Devon did. When I went to pick Devon up from Jackson's house, Jackson had cut Devon's hair off. I had shaped Devon's hair in a Mohawk style and given Devon an "S Curl." I purposely did not cut Devon's hair because it was too soon after the "S Curl." When I went to pick up Devon from Jackson's house, he had cut all of Devon's hair off, had made Devon strip down to his underwear, and whipped him so bad that Devon had to be taken to the emergency room. That was not the first time Jackson had severely beaten Devon. Once before, Devon took a razor blade and slashed a picture of Jackson's oldest daughter. I felt that Devon was just a kid, but Jackson commences beating Devon. He beat Devon so bad that I stepped in, telling Jackson not to hit Devon again. Jackson immediately responded, "This is my son." Devon fell on the bed, and I grabbed the belt away from Jackson and told him, "That was enough." I left Jackson for seven days, and the blisters from the beating he had given Devon lasted about seven days as well.

When I took Devon to the emergency room, doctors treating Devon called the police, the social worker, and the Department of Health and Human Services. The police wanted to charge Jackson with felony child abuse. However, a charge of felony child abuse would have made Jackson lose his job, and I did not want that to happen. Jackson was barred from seeing Devon for at least one year. When the year ended, the court authorized him to spend time with Devon. He picked Devon up and took him to the rodeo and his home. Jackson's wife told him that she did not want Devon at their home, and Jackson only spent two to three hours with his son. Jackson maybe saw his son two or three times in four years. The last time he saw Devon was at Clarice's house, Jackson's mother and Devon's grandmother.

CHAPTER ELEVEN

"My Psycho Ex"

NICOLLETTE:

I am from Arkansas, Little Rock, Arkansas. I grew up impoverished. We lived in projects, my grandmother lived in the projects, and my mother lived in the projects. A significant portion of my family lived in a project, and at that time, it was the eighties and nineties, so drugs were rampant. It was just an awful time growing up, and my dad was never there. My stepfather raised me; he was a drug addict and an alcoholic who abused my mother and brother. Therefore, I became very protective of my brother. So, I would start to stand up against my stepfather and physically fight him. It became highly chaotic until I ended up moving out of the home at age eighteen.

My brother moved in with me for a couple of years to finish high school, so we lived together so he could get away from that stepfather of mine. So growing up was tough. But I was always a little different from everybody else. I've never really had friends. I've always stayed to myself, so I used to say, "I've never seen anything extraordinary, but I know it's something out there different." I just knew that I was not in my chosen environment. I just knew it. My first job was an apprenticeship in a medical laboratory; I did well in high school. My professor contacted my mother and said, "You need to make sure your daughter becomes an engineer." I didn't even know what engineering was and did not pay that much attention to what my professor said. More or less, I thought,

Oh, whatever. So my mom kept that in her mind, and at the same time, engineering is mostly math, so I had a white math teacher, and I'm in high school, and she asked me, "What do you want to do when you go to college?" I told her engineering, and she said, "Oh no, that's way too hard for you. No, you will not be able to keep up with the math."

Well, long story short, I went to college and got that engineering degree, and I went back to high school looking for that woman. At that point, she had already retired. So, whatever, Ms. McDonald. But after I left home at eighteen, moving forward, I was just on my own, literally, like navigating through life on my own. And when I graduated from college, I felt like I graduated from college, got everything now, and wanted to have a family. I wanted to be married. And so, yeah, I'm now getting into him-- so yeah, that's pretty much my upbringing.

Now, how would I define domestic abuse? Domestic abuse is anyone who forcefully inflicts or enforces their ways upon another person against that person's will. That is abuse, domestic abuse. In my opinion, domestic abuse isn't just physical; it can be mental or emotional. It's all of it. But, you know, society only recognizes the physical. Yes, that's how I would define it. I was in an abusive marriage. Well, before we even got married, I started seeing the signs that he was offensive, but, being young, navigating through life on my own, and not knowing what love is, I just thought, *Oh God, he loves me like that*.

So what happened? We were at his apartment, and he lived in Florida; I'm in Little Rock and took a flight to see him. And I don't know what happened, but we kind of got to tussling. I mean, like kind of fussing, and he grabbed my arm and scratched it real bad, and I ran into the bathroom. I tried to slam the door, and he pushed it in. And then we were kind of arguing; he grabbed me from the bathroom. He took my suitcase, and he threw stuff everywhere. And I was like, I don't know. That was the first time in retrospect I realized like this man was crazy.

Where did I meet this crazy person? Online. I met him, believe it or not, on a website called interracial dating.com. That's when I was going through my feelings of being tired of abusive Black men or just Black men who don't have it together. So I wanted to step outside the box. I was young and out of my mind then. But, he was Black, and he was on the website too; and that's how we met.

But I met my husband online because it got to where I didn't know where to meet a man. Where you go, what you do? I didn't want to go to a bar or a club. What do you do? It was so many people that were in my situation. How do you meet somebody? So, you go to a reputable online dating site and see if you can meet somebody. The whole situation was a little different because we met online. We came to see each other a few times, and we decided three months in that we would get married. However, I wanted to wait at least until we hit the one-year mark. So even though we agreed on three months, we didn't officially get married. He was living in Florida, and I was in someplace else. So over the phone, there weren't many quarrels. It was just more so in person when things would get weird, you know, crazy. And, another thing is his friends warned me not to marry him, his best friend. Best friend, to this day, warned me. His best friend said, "Don't do it." And again, people don't understand. I was lonely in my life. I didn't have my mother or father; I didn't have anybody navigating through the world with me. I just wanted to be married.

He was a Christian Black man. You know, he was a Christian Black man. So I felt like he was taking care of everything, even though he had two children. You know he was a truck driver, an over-the-road truck driver. And, compared to the type of men I had been meeting up to that point, I felt like he was perfect. At the time, he wasn't insecure about my status, you know, so I was just like this will work, but all the signs were there everything. People warned me; he warned me through his behavior. It just got to the point that we had decided we were going to get married. I had invested so much. I paid for the wedding. I had invested so much money into it, which I just said, "I'm just going to go through with it, instead of just losing all the money," because, by the time we got close to the marriage, I felt like I was making kind of a mistake. But I felt like I had already committed to this whole thing. So, yeah.

When we would meet in person, there were no triggers that would make him angry, no specific things that would make him angry. A lot of the time, you wouldn't even know. You wouldn't even know that any particular item or action would upset him. In the beginning, he wasn't nearly as controlling as he became. At first, he loved the fact that I was very flashy at that time: I wore my heels, I wore my big hair, whatever he loved. After we got married, he wanted to strip me of all of that, all of Lettie, and he wanted to get rid of her so that no one else could see me. You know what I mean. So, when we were together, I don't recall many events that stand out because we were not together a lot. We weren't together a lot because he was in Florida and I was in Little Rock. You know I worked, he worked, so it wasn't even like we could meet, physically, a lot, but I just recalled that specific incident because that's when I realized like okay. I thought, and I know this is crazy, but maybe it's just that he loves me that much.

After we got married, we decided, okay, first of all, on my wedding day, I was so depressed. I was so miserable because I didn't want to go through with it. But everybody was there, and I just felt committed. So after we got married, I remember walking away from the reception crying the dark tears from the depths of my soul. You know, I was just hoping I had not ruined my life. I did not respect him at this point. I knew that being with him was going to depreciate my life. I just knew it, but at the same time, I had no one else. No one else to help me kind of see my worth and see that this is deeper than just you marrying someone who's beneath you or not on your level. This is about the fact that you're about to go through something that you never fathom that you would ever go through. But, you know, it wasn't there, it didn't happen. I married him, and I think it started on the honeymoon. The craziness began on the honeymoon.

He was just so controlling. He wanted to tell me how I should dress or what I should say, how I should eat. And, I've always been very, like, defensive. I'm going to defend myself no matter what. So when he would try to do that, it would always create conflicts because I'm, like, "You married me. You didn't know me to know me, but you knew enough about the basics of me and my life to know I am who I am." You know, so I started to see on the honeymoon that this was just going to go left. We went to Hawaii. I paid for it. And I just knew that from that moment on, this was about to be something terrible.

We stayed married for about a year and a half. I couldn't take it anymore because of the way he treated me. I'm shocked I made it even that long. This man was a monster. He's a monster. And it's so funny because talking to his friends, like I'm still close, not close, but I'm still really cool with his two best friends because they're the ones that warned me. They love him, and they are loyal to him, but they respected me enough to realize and tell me, "You don't deserve this; let me warn you." For that, I've always appreciated them, and they knew that their friend was crazy. You see, they didn't want to flat out say, "Don't do it, he's crazy," but they didn't want me to get hurt by him, so I've always had respect for them so we could keep in touch, maybe once a year or whatever. When I spoke to one of them, he told me, "He is still the same." His friend said, "Leopards don't change their spots. He is still the same."

They warned me that he was not used to being with "your type of woman." They told me I was different from any woman he had ever had and not to marry him. Now, in retrospect, I realized, he's used to women with lesser means than what I had. He was used to trash, and that was what I was not. He was used to another type of woman, and he was used to being in the breadwinning position with women who had lesser means than he. And he was neither with me.

When I tried telling him about how I felt, oh my goodness, not only did I try to say to him about how I felt. I took us to multiple counselors, therapists, and a pastor. His father, his mother. Oh, yes. Yes, I tried everything. That's why when I finally made my decision to get divorced. I was at peace with the decision because if I didn't do anything else. I tried to make that brutal marriage work. I tried.

I survived the marriage as long as I did because I had to. I don't remember good times with him. I remember he didn't really like people or crowds. And I've always been the type I love to go to excellent restaurants. I especially loved to be outdoors and around people. And I liked to try different restaurants in the area, and he only wanted to go to Golden Corral because it's cheaper and you can get everything you want. That was the problem. He had a poor man syndrome. He grew up even more impoverished than I. He grew up under a lot of mental distress and mental abuse, and he was put out at a very young age and had to navigate his way; it was just a mess. Not to mention his father is naturally aggressive like he is. His father was vulgar and disrespectful. But, at the same time to strangers, they present themselves very well, you know, because he was just like that. Yeah.

When we were in counseling, he would always say that everything wrong in his life was my fault. I mean, like he had two kids, two sons, that he didn't see because the women were terrified of him. There had been two different women, and both of them, in the middle of the night, or when he was gone, packed up everything and ran. He didn't know where these people were for years, both of them. And guess what I did? I packed up my stuff in the middle of the day and ran to Memphis, Tennessee.

Looking back, I think that what I could have done differently that might have improved my situation would have been to listen to everything people had been telling me, like, "This is not what you want," or "We know what you want, but you won't find that, and you will certainly not find that in him." I've been to jail because of this man, and I've had the police called. I don't know how many times I can't even count. I paid for everything in the marriage, throughout the marriage. He was physically well. He tried to be physically violent, but I will always fight back. It would just be physical fights. And it was always teardowns, and he became jealous of me, so jealous of me because I was able to do everything for us, and he wasn't, even though I didn't care that he wasn't. You know, I was like, "Just do the best that you can." And he was just angry because the type of things that I wanted to do just reminded him so significantly of what he does not have.

You know, and so I'm never going to forget when we first moved to North Carolina. We moved to North Carolina. And I had a beautiful apartment. Oh, it was so beautiful. You know, but it was pretty pricey, like $1,000 a month at that time. And it had everything. And so after that year, we decided we are going to get something just a little bit cheaper, so we found this house. At this point, he hadn't even been working, and he had finally got a job, and he was getting his first paycheck. My ex knew I would use the money from my paycheck to get the truck to move our stuff to the new house.

When I went to pick him up from work that man got in the car and I was like, "Okay, do you have the money?" You know, he cursed me out so bad. "You just want to take all my money. I just got paid, etc." Meanwhile, I'm sitting there like, but you knew how we needed to spend the money. Long story short, we get into a fight, and the police get called. And I am never going to forget when I was just sitting there, sitting in the truck, like eventually, I got the truck myself. And I was sitting there, and the cop was like, "If you don't leave this man, this man will get you in some bad trouble." The policeman said I've seen men like him before. Because one thing about my ex-husband, when he gets around the police, he performs. Like, he wants them to side with him. So he was going to be extra animated, you know, just really dramatic and exaggerate. You know, what he could do to make me look crazy. I don't do all of those animations and dramas, but it doesn't mean that I'm not telling the truth. So the police, most of the time, would side with him. And I got to the point where he was like, "I own you." The police made him feel that power over me. I own you, you know, and so it was, it was terrible. All I recall was our fights, like fights.

I remember like some Saturdays; he would wake up first thing in the morning and watch football all day. And so, I remember I would ask if he would take me to a movie. His response, "No, I'll be watching football." You know, it's just like utterly emotional abuse, mental abuse, and physical abuse. I worked every day and would clean up the house when I would come home and cook. I cooked, I cleaned up, and I would go to bed. I wake up in the morning, he'd been up all night, so the whole house was just a mess. The kitchen, everything, was just a mess. He wouldn't work, you know, and if he did work, he only wanted to work at Walmart or AutoZone, like very mediocre jobs. And I remember he knew how to clean cars and clean them like it was nothing to it. He did not need a lot to do it. He could have a couple of things, a rag, or whatever. He could detail the crap out of a car. He was so good. And I was like, "I would invest in that form of a business if you do it." "No, I don't want to do that." He would make up excuses—"No, don't I want to do this or that."

Now, I was like, "Okay, well, how about I go back to school, get a master's degree, so maybe I can make more money?" His response, "Why you got to get all of the education?" I said, "Why you won't go?" Response, "Because I got child support, I got to pay." Like, the man was just hateful, just mean and mad, all the time.

And then there was this other time. This one, I would never in my life, forget. I had what was going around at that time—strep throat. I was so sick. I had strep throat. And I asked him; I was like, "Can you please go to the store and get me some Lysol because I'm just sitting here. I am not feeling well and soaking up germs from my illness, and I'm not getting better. Can you please?" He said, "Okay, all right after this game, after this game." I'm like, "Okay, I'm waiting hours and hours." Oh, I'm asking, "Could you please go?" His response, "After the game." Okay. He won't go. So, I finally got up, put my clothes on, and I went. I was so sick. When I came back, no, he didn't say, "Give me the Lysol; I'll spray the bed down." I said, "If you don't get the 'F' away from me. I don't need you to do this."

At this point, I'd already done the hard part. You know. We got into a physical fight. Physical fight, because I told this fool he was not spraying down that bed, and I meant that -- a physical fight. That was my life. I gained a ton of weight. Although I stayed married only one and a half years, it seemed much longer. I had stopped being flashy; I was plain. He just stripped me of all the life I had in me. You have no idea of the events that took place within that short year and a half. We were--wait, wait, we were saying in one place, a home rental, and the home had a boat in the parking lot. And I remember one day, he got mad and took my phone from me because he didn't want me to have it. I was going to meet my girlfriend. He didn't want me to go, so he took my phone from me. I was trying to get my phone back. We were on the porch. He pushed me with all his strength. I flew off the porch, and my body hit the side of that boat. To this day, one of my hips is just a little bigger than the other because the inflammation never completely went down. I still have that scar. I mean, it was a huge, huge bruise on the entire side of my body.

The finale got me to the point where I was just like, I can't, and I can't do this anymore. We had been staying in separate rooms, not dealing with each other in any capacity for like four months. But before our falling out, I purchased us – for Christmas— a package deal that was available at that time. And I said, "I'll purchase this now, and we'll have it for Christmas, and there was no refund." So I purchased this package deal for a trip to Florida, and I mean the flights and everything, and you know it's like you can't change the name. So, we didn't talk for four months, didn't deal with each other, but then Christmas came around, and I'm like, "Listen, I got this package. I can't, you know, take anyone else because everything is in your name, you know, and so if you want to go, you can; if not, that's fine, I'm still going to go." So he's like, "We can go." So I'm thinking, *You would think that you know you haven't dealt with somebody; you don't talk to them. You're married, and you're about to go on the trip.* I thought this would be an opportunity to try to repair things. "No." This man, long story short, ended up fighting me on the freeway.

It was terrible; we pulled over on the freeway to fight. I am telling you, my ex was crazy.

The fight started this way. My mother called me on the phone, and my sister was also on the phone. My mother started telling me things about my sister's boyfriend because my sister's boyfriend wasn't right. My ex-husband was listening, and he chimed in, saying, "There are two sides to every story; you all just telling this one side." I said, "Listen, this doesn't have anything to do with you. Please don't overstep your boundary." And so then I went back to talking to my family, and next thing you know, he pulled over on the side of the freeway and jumped out of the car yelling, "F" and your raggedy-ass family. My mother and sister were on the phone, and I told them, "I am so sorry." But, I promise you, I promise you, if I don't promise you anything else, this will be the last time that you ever have to deal with this. I promise you that. And so, I got off the phone with them. He came back in a car, talking junk, and we started physically fighting. And, the sickest part is when we pulled over, another car pulled over. And, in this car was a pastor. And so he went up to the car, talking off biblical or whatever. And then the pastor gave him like a pamphlet or something to come to the church. And he came back as nothing had happened. I couldn't believe it. I just couldn't believe my eyes. You know, I was like, this man is the devil.

So it was this one time where he wanted to fight. And he got close to my face. I hate to say it, but he was foaming at the mouth like white stuff was coming out as well; he was crazy. I remember looking in his eyes; there was nothing there. It was just darkness. When I watched TV and heard people describing an encounter with somebody who almost killed them, they would always say his eyes. His eyes were black. When they say it, I would say, "Oh my God, I know what it means to look in a person's eyes, and the eyes show nothing but meanness."

You know in your heart that person is ready to kill you. The eyes appear black, as though something else is guiding them. Their eyes are just black. And that's when I knew this man got something in him. Look at this. I was scared of him, and I started walking back a little bit of backing up. I was saying, "Get out of my face. Get out of my face," and I was looking for something just in case I had to grab something because his eyes were black. I don't know; I just wanted to tell that one.

And I got to tell you this one, please. Another reason I knew that this man had evil attached to him. This man had sin attached to him. When he finally started working, when he would leave early in the morning, like four or five o'clock, when he would depart, I would go back to sleep every time he went. And it's like, spirits in my sleep would attack me. Every time this man left the house, the spirits would attack me, and it got to the point where I was terrified to go to sleep. I was scared. I would try to stay up and keep lights on everything because when I slept, the same thing will happen. In my dreams, it would be in the same room, the same everything in my dreams. And I started hearing a bunch of whispers. I would keep my door closed. But, I heard sounds outside the door, and I would get scared because I knew it was them, and they were just entities; you can't see them. You can't say, "Oh, I see this face." There were no faces. It's just—they are just entities. You just know they're there, and one would come and claw at me, although he didn't have nails. You just know that is what he was doing to you, and I don't even know if the entity was a he or it. I just know it would claw at me. I remember standing, screaming in the blood of Jesus and just saying, "You can't destroy me." I went through this every day. And even though I would fight these entities back, nobody knew how this felt; I was terrified—scared, like afraid, I can't explain it. I know they were attached to him because when I moved away from that man, which has never happened to me since. I've never had another experience like that before. And I felt, that oh, this man had demons attached to him.

That man, that's why he's evil, and he hates women because of his momma. His momma put him out. You know his mother put him out and put another man, what he felt like another man, before his daddy. He hated women, and he hated me. He hated me so much. When I finally moved out, which was after that Florida trip, he left me in Florida. He ended up coming back home, and I didn't care. I stayed there the whole seven days and had a good time by myself. And when I got home,

I finally came home, and I remember he wasn't there, and I was so sleepy. I waited for a while and then went to bed. And then, I heard banging on the door, and I went, and I opened the door. And, there he stood yelling, "Why the 'F'? You lock the door," and so on. Mind you, I had not seen or heard from this man in seven days since a fight in Florida where he left me. And this is what he does the minute I open that door and when he went crazy like that. I went back to my room. And I said, "I stared at the ceiling." And I said, "God, please. I'm only twenty-eight years old, God; I'm not eighty-two; please don't let this be my final destination. Please don't." And that Monday came, I went to work, and I was at my computer just crying to myself, and my brother called me. I told my brother that I didn't know what to do because in the state where I was, you got to be separated a year before you can be divorced, and I can't be with this monster anymore. And my brother said, "Go back to Little Rock. Go back to Little Rock, where you got married, and get your divorce there. It's only a four-month process." I was like, what? My brother said, "Yeah, you need a lawyer." I got one.

By the end of the conversation with the lawyer, I had paid him my $1,200, and everything just started rolling. I couldn't believe it. I couldn't believe it was moving that fast. So I came home, feeling like a boulder lifted off me. And I told him, I said, "Listen. You will receive divorce papers. I want to let you know so that you don't be surprised, but I am getting a divorce." And what did he do? He got up, walked off, and slammed the door in my face. I said, "Okay." So I remember I went to work the next day. And I said I couldn't stay in the house with this man, not another minute, and I just can't. So I started looking online for places to stay, places for rent. And I found this one duplex, and everything inside this duplex was brand new; the previous people who stayed there destroyed it. So the owner had to replace everything. It was a two-bedroom, perfect, actual apartment. And guess what I did? I put down my down payment for that place.

And I came home, and I told him, I'm never going to forget; at this point, it was like January the fifth, maybe. And I told him, "On February

1st, I will be out of here." And we had three months left on the lease to that place, and we're both saying that. And I said, "I'd let you know that I'm going to continue to pay the bills here because my name is attached to this. You know I pay for everything, right?" So I said, "I'm going continue to pay the bills here for three months, but after three months, you are on your own." And I meant that. I had planned to leave the utilities on and everything, but you could not have services in multiple locations in my state. So, I had to get the lights cut off at that house, so he was there in the dark. And he went crazy; he started stalking me and found out where I lived. To this day, I don't know how he found out. I don't know how he found out where I lived, but he found out where I live. He was stalking me, calling me; he was going crazy. He was losing weight. It got scary. It got to the point where I was like, "Letta, he's probably going to do, 'if I can't have you, nobody can,' threat." It was getting scary. This man treated me like trash the entire marriage. And now he'd, he'd lost control, and so he was going crazy. And that's when my mama said, -- I remember he came to my house, and he was going crazy. So, my mama called, and I was going crazy because he was stressing me out. And he was like, "Let me talk to her."

So my mama ended up calling him on his phone. And she convinced him to leave. My mama called me back a few hours later and was like, "You know, I've been on the phone with him for three hours." She said, "You have got to go because I'm scared he might kill you." And I said, "Okay." Within two weeks, I had found another job in Memphis, Tennessee. And I tried to sneak in and pack all my stuff, and he popped up at my house, saw U-Haul, and saw I was packing. And he was like, "You just going to leave? Are you just going to leave? You owe me to at least tell me you are leaving." I said, "I don't owe you anything." I was trying to hurry up and leave because I didn't want him to know I was going, and then he would try and kill me. You know, that's why I was trying to sneak in and do it, but I did it. And I've never looked back. I have never looked back.

You know, I heard from his psycho behind a few years ago, when his mom died. I've called him to, you know, to give him my condolences.

And no, this fool didn't say, "I don't want you to call me anymore. "Call you anymore?" I don't call you. I just called you today. "Well, I don't think you should call me no more, because I'm still in love with a woman who's going to marry somebody else" and blah blah blah. I said, "Okay, well, you take care, and I'm sorry about what happened to your mama." And I got off the phone. I couldn't. Before we divorced, my grandmother died, and I was extremely close to her. She was everything to me. Do you know that man had a physical fight with me on the freeway the day before her funeral because I didn't want to go with him to get a haircut? Did I need to find a dress to wear to my grandma's funeral? He had a physical fight with me on the day before the funeral. I couldn't believe it. And to this day, I believe my grandmother, when she died, her spirit was like, "Oh no, I'm going to clean this mess up," so six months later, I was divorced. Six months after she died, I was divorced from that monster.

I paid for everything in the marriage because we had to live. My ex-husband would not work consistently after the wedding, and when he did work, he was only making a minimum wage. He's only willing to give this much; you still got to survive. You know, I remember this one time I had some chicken, some fast-food chicken or something, and I wouldn't say I like to put my chicken in a microwave because it gets soggy. I wanted to put it in an oven to make it a little crispy, but it was only a few pieces, and no, he didn't say, "Cut that oven off. You are about to run up the bill like that for a couple of pieces of chicken." I said, "Who pays the bill?" I couldn't believe it. We got into the most prominent argument, a yelling match over that because he's telling me that I can't use the oven. I paid for the stove. Who, who, oh, who does this. He was a monster. And it was so bad that even his sister would tell me, "Girl, leave him." His family started saying get away from him because they knew he was crazy, and they knew I wasn't. I was defending myself. I always protected myself against this psycho.

I would say to anyone in an abusive relationship, what helped me, when I think about it, was during the four months when he was living his own life, and I was living mine. I joined some online forums with other people who were in abusive relationships. And I met this one girl; we talked for weeks. Her husband was psychotic, and she was Caucasian, and he was Caucasian. My husband was psychotic, he was African American, and I was African American. I bonded with her, and it just goes to show that race does not matter. I never knew whatever happened to her. But, just talking to other people who are going through it will make you realize you are human, you're not experiencing something super new, and you're not alone. That helped me.

You have to ask yourself a question, especially when you are a young adult, but it does not matter your age. I don't care if you're eighty years old. Ask yourself, do you want to spend your last days with this being your legacy? Do you want to spend the rest of your life miserable? Ask yourself, is it worth it? Ask yourself if your mother and father come together in love to bring you on this earth to be with someone who will destroy your life. You got to figure out how to love yourself. I couldn't do this; I could not stay in that relationship. I had to leave; I know it's scary.

Because of intertwining lives with a significant other, the first steps are always frightening. You don't know where to start. What if you get out there and you don't make it? You don't know, and it can't get any worse than that. You are with that person. So that's what I would say try to reach out to other people. For the inspiration to just know like, Okay, first of all, I'm not alone. Second of all, what can I do, you know, where I can start and talk to other people who will help me answer some of those questions? Then, love yourself enough to get the courage actually to take some action. You know and do something, and realize you don't do something now. You probably won't survive today to do anything later because he might kill you.

When I came back from Florida, I went to lunch with my girlfriend. And I told her the entire story, like all of it. And I got to the part where I said, "So he left, and I had a good time." And she said, "What you mean he left?" "You mean he left, like left the room and went and got a drink, or got another room, left how?" I'm like, "No, he flew back to North

Carolina." And so she said, "Oh, Nicollette. Do you hear yourself?" I'm like, "No, what's the problem?" She's like, "That's not right."

"What, he left you there. First of all, he fought you, had the police get involved, and then he left you in Florida." I didn't think about that because I was so happy that he went; I didn't, I didn't think anything was a problem, but then when I thought about it, I was like, what husband does that though? Get a whole free trip? He doesn't have to contribute a dime because I paid for the trip. "For what, for him to physically fight me, disrespect my family, and then get the police involved and leave you. Just leave you there." And that's when I started thinking about my marriage like I am in such a hole. And I found a way to normalize or not normalize but just accept what he did to me. I mean, like just deal with it, instead of seeing how bad, like, this is bad. I just felt we found a way to just deal with it, you know. I mean, the man ripped my pants off me one time, rip them in half, and tore them from my body. He did it in a way where he didn't pull me down or anything. I was still standing. That's how his strength was with me. He just ripped my jeans off me.

My same girlfriend. I'm never going to forget this one either. She came over, and we had all ordered some wings. We had some drinks, and he invited one of his friends over. We had some honey barbecue. And, I don't remember if I had asked him, "Could he put me some up?" or if there were any more, or, I don't know what I said. But that man went crazy.

And my girlfriend was looking, with her eyes wide open. And I was kind of happy she saw it so that she could see what I was trying to tell her I got through. And he just went off, and we got the arguing. And finally, she said, "Okay, so let's go to the store, you know, like, to cool off." And she was like, "Oh my God that is scary." I'm like, I know, that is what I deal with, a psychotic fool, somebody you don't even know goes off about something like this, take it to go from zero to a hundred for no reason. Yes. In another weakness, we used to go to this church, and the pastor, who also doubled as our therapist, you know, our counselor, trying to help us. And I remember we were at church one day, and my ex had this thing where he felt like he knew everything. He was a specialist in everything; even if you were a specialist in the area, he knows more stuff about it than you. He was a know-it-all. And we were eating with a couple of other people. There was another couple. The woman paid for everything because she was the only one working in the relationship, and the couple had gotten an income tax refund. The man in the couple told the woman that he should get a part of the income tax refund. My crazy ex-husband jumped in and said, "Well, he does deserve half of it, because dah, dah, dah, dah, dah," giving his opinion, and I think I said something like, "Nobody asked you, who do you think you are?"

And so, he started standing up and getting louder and louder. And I'm never going to forget, everybody got up and walked out of the restaurant. They got up and walked out because he frightened them. And me, I was so used to this that I was not frightened; I was going to fight back. I was embarrassed. I remember leaving and getting in the car. We got into a physical fight in the church parking lot. The church parking lot, and I remember he got out the car, and was like, told me to suck his you know what, and "F" me. I got in the car, closed the door, and drove off. And so, a couple of hours later, the pastor brought him home. And I had put his stuff on the front porch. And he came in the house, trying to argue, and they try to calm him down, and he tried to take my key and throw it in a pond, just psychotic stuff. And I remember the pastor spent so long trying to help us. The last time, the pastor said to us, he looked at us with such exhausted eyes. He was so tired of us. And he said, "You all need to separate." This pastor was a man who is 1,000 percent pro-marriage would never; you just know that that's not something he would ever be quick to recommend. He was tired of us because he always had to come to mediate to try and make things right for us. And anytime he did, all my husband would say is, "She this, she that, she this, she that." And I tried to change it up a bit like I would say, "Okay, I do these things, or this is what I do." And he would jump in, "Yes, she does this, and she does that, on and on." He never took accountability for anything and blamed me for everything wrong in his life. And when the pastor said,

"Yes, you all need to separate," I knew then, Oh yeah, oh yeah, I would get out of this marriage. No more. I was humiliated when the pastor told us we should break apart. When a pastor tells you that you should separate in a marriage, you already know it's terrible.

Through it all, I feel that I have recovered from the abuse he put me through. My abusive relationship was brutal, and it was a devastating time. When I got out of it, I didn't know who I was. I didn't know what I liked. I didn't know how to wear heels anymore. I'm never going to get it when I was walking around my house practicing wearing heels again because I just completely stopped being so busy trying to survive, but it was like learning me all over again. I remember when I was in my new place, and I was like, "Well, Nicollette, what do you like? What do you want to do, like, I don't know?" I don't know, and I don't know me anymore.

My point in saying this is that once I got back to being myself again, once I, you know, reestablished myself, I finally met my husband today. It made me appreciate him so much because he is 180 degrees different from that monster. It made me understand gentleness, somebody who recognizes what love is to see somebody who cares about you. You know, it just made me appreciate it, and I think if I hadn't gone through that, I probably wouldn't have enjoyed it as much as I do now, or as much as I do now and as much as I did when I met my husband.

The one thing that I can say about my psycho ex is that he was not a cheater. He was beyond loyal. He wouldn't mess with another woman, and if he told another woman that he was married and she continued to pursue him, he would go off. He did not play those games; he did not like cheating. Cheating was very, very offensive for him to do it or for me. So, I can say that he was psychotically loyal to me.

What I went through with my ex-husband has caused me to have some post-traumatic stress. You know, going to jail and spending two days locked up, a no call, no show in your career. I don't work in McDonald's. I'm an electrical engineer, a no call, no show only to have to go back to work and tell your boss I was in jail. I stayed in a town where they put your picture in the paper, along with your name where you lived when you get arrested.

So, they started talking about me. So one of my girlfriends came and told me like, "Yes, they are talking about you." So, you know what I did. I went right over to all of them was like, "Yes, I went to jail. Yes, because I thought of my husband. Yes. Anything you need to know, ask me; you all don't have to whisper or wonder I don't mind telling you about it." And they were just so blown away that I did that, and they were like, "What, you are okay?" I said, "Do I look like I am hurt? I am wonderful. So you guys don't have to sit amongst each other and talk. Just ask me, I'll let you know." And I walked away. But even though I didn't show that I was embarrassed, I was humiliated. I was offended, just embarrassed in every respect, every regard. It was not like people didn't know. I had gone to jail. Now, I had to tell my boss the situation not to consider reporting me to human resources; this was just terrible, and I had to deal with it.

And then I told you I was from the projects, right. I will not tell you before we moved out of the apartment in North Carolina into the house that was a little cheaper. This fool said, "Well, we don't just move to the projects and save some money." Did I say moved to where? I said, "So, I fought my way out of the projects, and put myself through school, and got my career, only to end up in the same spot I started." I knew then, this man? I said, "Oh God, no." This man is just; he is just a bum. This man will hold me back. He will hold me back and destroy what I've accomplished. He would always make me feel like my accomplishments were nothing. And then when he told me, he said Florida's education school system produces more educated children. And I was like, "Well, you know Little Rock doesn't do the best, but it does what it does," and he's like, "No Florida's, it's way better." And I was like, "If Florida does so much better, what happened to you?" He got so mad at me, and he started calling me names and his child's mother; she's just pure trash, lives in a trailer park with like seven or eight other people, dogs with mange and fleas, all coming in and out, just junk. So he's going to say to me, she's better than you, dah, dah, dah, dah-- to insult me, and that did.

I can't believe I let that insult me; that's so stupid, but it did. We ended up getting into a whole physical fight over that. And I'm not going to tell you. We were in Raleigh, North Carolina; at that time, we were at a hotel because it was a tropical storm, back in our hometown, so I took us to Raleigh to get a hotel so we wouldn't be there without power, and this is what happened. He was psycho, just psycho, just psychotic. Oh my God. It was a good fight because he wanted to talk about school systems, for what? Who cared?

I know I should have recognized any warning signs. But, to me, they were not there during the first three months. More of the abusive signs manifested once the wedding planning started. It wasn't within three months. It was when the wedding planning began, or approximately two months before the wedding. I was like, "Oh God, oh boy, what have I done?" What am I doing, you know, but he had already relocated from Florida to Little Rock at that point. It was no longer like I could say do not call me anymore. I invested so much. The entire wedding was more than $12,600; I paid for it and was only twenty-six or twenty-seven years old. The amount of money invested was too much to throw away or just walk away.

Now, I would tell that same girl. If you don't walk away from that money, girl, you will make ten times more than that over your lifetime. Walk away from that mess. But, at the time, that's not how I felt, and that is not what I was thinking. I know that I will never be able to fully express in its entirety the impact that my abusive marriage had on my life. I can give people an excellent understanding, make people feel reasonably satisfied. But, you can never make someone fully understand. For a person to truly understand abuse, you would have to experience it. That is why it's essential to talk to other people who have experienced abuse in their own life experiences because only they understand. Those who have suffered abuse need someone to listen to them as they tell their stories. Those who have not experienced abuse are more likely to be entertained; to them, it may be just a story that they're engaged by, but a victim or somebody in the situation that not just a story, they feel what I feel, they know. They have been in a similar situation.

My story evokes emotions in them that only I and they understand. I don't think one would ever be able to explain it thoroughly, but I think you can explain it well enough for someone else to see and say, "Well, that was or is a toxic situation."

CHAPTER TWELVE

PARALLELS OF DARKNESS AND LIGHT

Faith Etiquette: "Now, faith is the substance of things hoped for, the evidence of things not seen."

Hebrews 11:1 (KJV)

<u>The Seesaw Impact</u>:

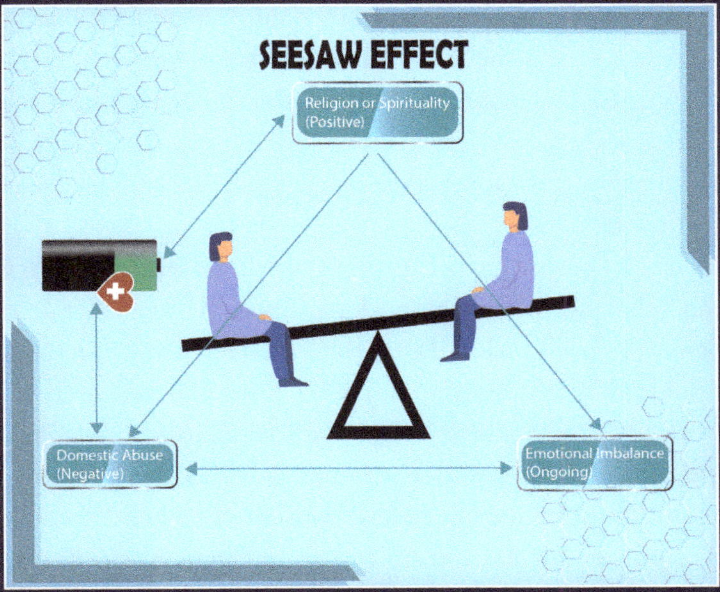

As children, Anna and Deanna would take the longest old plank of wood they could find, usually a plank that had fallen from their old wooden structured home, and place it on a tree stump. Anna would climb on one end of the plank of wood and Deanna on the other. They would hold on with their hands firmly gripping the sides of the old planks, being as careful as possible not to get the sharp fragments of the wood in their hands, and they would ride that plank of wood up and down. Joyful, then afraid, balanced, then off-balance, splinters of wood in hands that would not come out for days, hard bumps to the ground, and softer bumps off the ground. Whatever the ride was on the seesaw, Anna or Deanna could ever feel secure. Anna and Deanna had faith that the old plank would hold steady, and they would survive the ups and downs, even with the fragments. But the problem was that Anna and Deanna never knew how hard or soft the bumps might get or at what point they would fall from the plank, regardless of how tight they held on. And, if they did fall, what would happen? How hard would the fall be? How much pain can one endure? How many tears or what joy might that old seesaw bring.

Nonetheless, Anna and Deanna would keep going up and down, up and down. That is the life of victims of domestic abuse. Regardless of their religion or spiritual endurance, they will continue forever on the endless seesaw ride. That seesaw ride serves as an equalizer for women suffering from abusive relationships. A continuous seesaw ride is problematic.

The impact of abuse, whether physical, mental, emotional, or verbal, cause an imbalanced life that is nothing short of a miracle, a miraculous intervention, woven within the precious fabric, sewn within the soul of all humankind that can stamp out what Anna believed to be a severe mental illness. Many studies have sought to explain domestic abuse, violence, and survival. However, few studies have looked at domestic abuse and endurance related to an heir of continued existence from both a positive and a negative spectrum with a fundamental seesaw effect on the victim. In an abusive domestic environment, positive and negative forces align with a horizontal axis that seesaws between religion, spirituality, abuse, and survival. Domestic abuse and violence, for some, is such a traumatizing event. It can cause severe emotional breakdown and imbalance. Research showed that abused victims began experiencing unexplained, extreme panic attacks years later, interrupting their healthy way of life. Some withdrew from reality by refusing to socialize with others to the point where they had to quit their jobs or become institutionalized. Others left home without providing a valid explanation to loved ones. Others just kept a façade, pretending to be okay while suffering and smothering inside and smiling on the outside. Yet, some others shunned family members who they believed did not help them during the trying times of abuse. Nearly all victims used religion, faith, or spirituality to balance or stabilize their lives to assimilate some form of normalcy when needed. However, the abuser often continued their abusive patterns.

Historically, differences and similarities raise questions relevant to individual decision-making and subsequent experiences within and outside one's control. African-American women, in particular, faced a higher risk of domestic violence than their white counterparts. The Violence Policy Center showed that men murdered black women at a rate of more than two and a half times higher than white women.

There is a time and place for everything, and there is nothing new under the sun. Therefore, it is no parallel between light and darkness. Light and darkness will always have the exact distance between them and will never meet. The light of Sanctity and the darkness of abuse are parallel, runs continuously, and will never meet.

As you read about the experiences or viewed survey results, try to imagine it's you, your mother, grandmother, daughter, granddaughter, child, sister, aunt, etc. No one deserves abuse, violence, or battering. Your home should be a place of refuge, your sanctuary, safe, untouched by the hands of abuse and violence. If only we had a magic crystal ball to view the future. We would solve, resolve, and address every perplexing, wicked, domestic abuse and violence challenge encountered. Some, if not all, before they happen, would be prevented. What about a magic pill, some magic formula that could tell us if we are likely to experience violence from an intimate partner? Unfortunately, there are no crystal balls, medications, or magic procedures to prevent domestic altercations. But, we do have indicators as findings from those who have experienced domestic abuse and violence. Voices of victims should not incur silence or marginalization; they should be listened to and embraced when and where possible.

To all the women and men who have suffered domestic abuse and are still suffering, to God be the glory. If you feel stuck in an abusive relationship, you do not have to remain as such. Although it's easier said than done, Anna was able to break free by the grace of God. According to Anna, it took a higher power than any power walking around on this earth. As humankind, we are all miracles. We are precious jewels enveloped within a unique treasure chest, filled with wonderful precious stones, and we should never let anyone take that away. "Let no one steal your joy."

New relationships bring challenges, but a new and better life is possible. "Keep hope alive." "Yes, you can." Those famous words were coined just for an abused victim to hear. Hope, keep it alive, and yes, you can have a new and better, abusive-free life; you owe it to yourself and your family to ensure that you do. The length of an abusive relationship does not matter. What matters most is what happens now. Start planning and maybe even praying or meditating today. Anna, Grace, Emma, Corona, Allison, and Nicolette were fortunate to get out of an abusive situation alive. Make a safety plan. Save a little money if you can, and for goodness sake, "Don't break down and tell your abuser about your plan." Finally, act as the Nike slogan suggests, and "Just Do It."

Biophysicist Pierre Lecomte du No, a Paris-born author and scientist, a former member of the Rockefeller Institute, and an officer in the French Army, believed that religion was the foundation of his scientific work. In the noted writing titled the *Divine Spark*, du No wrote that "from an evolution point of view, Nature's greatest invention is death." Although Dr. du No believed the future of man was bleak, and "humanity had not reached the age of reason," still, because humanity was the highest and most complex life form of all, we must continue developing in the direction of spirituality as Christ would have us to do.

Furthermore, "let every man remember that the destiny of humankind is incomparable and that it depends greatly on his will to collaborate in the transcendent task. And let him above all never forget that the divine spark is in him, alone, and that he is free to disregard it, to kill it, or to come closer to God by showing his eagerness to work with Him and for Him."

As we continue to think about our life and the lives of others, we should share our life stories. Domestic abuse and violence are complex and wicked problems, not easy to tame, and not well understood. Yet, we owe it to all humankind to better understand it and fix what we can, one home, one family, one community, and one nation, at a time, where possible.

"A gracious woman gets honor, and violent men get riches."
Proverbs 11:16 (English Standard Version)

"For what does it profit a man to gain the whole world and forfeit his soul."
Mark 8:36 (English Standard Version)

National Domestic Abuse Hotline:

1-800-799-7233

NOTES

About this Book

1. Carlson, B. E., & Worden, A. P. (2005). Attitudes and beliefs about domestic violence: Results of a public opinion survey: I. Definitions of domestic violence, criminal domestic violence, and vrevalence. *Journal of Interpersonal Violence*, *20*(10), 1197–1218. *https://doi.org/10.1177/0886260505278530.*

2. *King James Bible*. (n.d.) King James Bible Online. https://www.kingjamesbibleonline.org/ *(Original work published 1769).*

Preface

1. Albrecht, M. C. (1954). The relationship of literature and society. American *Journal of Sociology, 59*(5), 425-436. *https://doi.org/10.1086/221388.*

2. Cunningham, A. M. (2021, July 1). Canton woman's death spurs action on domestic violence regulations in Mississippi. *Mississippi woman's death puts focus on lack of domestic violence laws (clarionledger.com).*

Introduction

1. Carlson, B. E., & Worden, A. P. (2005). Attitudes and beliefs about domestic violence: Results of a public opinion survey:

1. Definitions of domestic violence, criminal domestic violence, and prevalence. *Journal of Interpersonal Violence, 20*(10), 1197–1218. https://doi.org/10.1177/0886260505278530.

2. Ashley, J. (1973). House of commons debates.

3. Collins, P. H. (2002). *Black feminist thought: Knowledge, consciousness, and the politics of empowerment*. Routledge.

4. Stolberg, G. S., & Hulse, C. (2019, April 25). Joe Biden expresses regret to Anita Hill, but she says I'm sorry is not enough. *Joe Biden Expresses Regret to Anita Hill, but She Says 'I'm Sorry' Is Not Enough - The New York Times (nytimes.com).*

Chapter One

1. Chodron, P. (2000). *When things fall apart*. Heart advice for difficult times. Shambhala Publications.

2. Wilson, K. J. (2005). *When violence begins at home: A comprehensive guide to understanding and ending domestic abuse*. Hunter House.

3. Hooker, J. (2016). Black lives matter and the paradoxes of US Black politics: From democratic sacrifice to democratic repair. *Political Theory, 44*(4), 448-469.

4. Shannon J. (2020, July 17). *'Black Lives Matter' isn't partisan or political, federal agency says (usatoday.com).*

5. MacDonald, H. (2016, April 27). The danger of the 'Black Lives Matter' movement. *https://www.manhattan-institute.org/html/danger-black-lives-matter-movement-8866.html.*

6. Violence Policy Center (2020, September). When men murder women: An analysis of 2018 homicide data. https://vpc.org/studies/wmmw2020.pdf

7. National Coalition against Domestic Violence (NCADV). Statistics. *https://www.ncadv.org/statistics#:~:text=1%20in%203%20women%20and%201%20in%204,have%20been%20injured%20by%20an%20intimate%20partner.%201.*

8. National Coalition against Domestic Violence (NCADV). Statistics. *https://www.ncadv.org/statistics#:~:text=1%20in%203%20women%20and%201%20in%204,have%20been%20injured%20by%20an%20intimate%20partner.%201.*

9. National Conference of State Legislatures (2019, June 13). Domestic violence/domestic abuse definitions and relationships. *https://www.ncsl.org/research/human-services/domestic-violence-domestic-abuse-definitions-and-relationships.aspx*

10. United Nations: (2020). International day for the elimination of violence against women November, 25. *https://www.un.org/en/observances/ending-violence-against-women-day.*

11. eNCa (2020, June 18). Ramaphosa on GBV: SA is fighting another pandemic. https://www.enca.com/news/ramaphosa-gbv-sa-fighting-another-pandemic.

12. Side Effects Public Media: WFYI-FM (2021, March 24). Domestic violence against Black women rising during pandemic. *Domestic Violence against Black Women Rising during Pandemic (wfyi.org).*

13. The Officer Down Memorial Page (2021). Officer Breann Rochelle Leath. *https://www.odmp.org/officer/24559-officer-breann-rochelle-leath*

14. Kercher, C., Swedler, D. I., Pollack, K. M., & Webster, D. W. (2013). Homicides of law enforcement officers responding to domestic disturbance calls. *Injury Prevention: Journal of the International Society for Child and Adolescent Injury Prevention, 19*(5), 331-5. https://doi.org/10.1136/injuryprev-2012-040723.

15. Jackson, W. (2020, May 18). 'You left before we were ready': JSU student killed in murder-suicide remembered. *https://www.clarionledger.com/story/news/2020/05/18/murder-suicide-pheonecia-ratliff-jackson-state-university-student-remembered/5208666002/.*

16. Marion, R., & McCarthy, W. (2018, November 10). Latasha Norman walk & run. *https://www.wlbt.com/2018/11/10/th-annual-latasha-norman-walkrun-held-honor-domestic-violence-victims/#:~:text=Norman%20was%20a%2020-year-old%20Jackson%20State%20University%20student,found%20in%20a%20wooded%20area%20in%20North%20Jackson.*

Chapter Two

1. Goodreads (2021, July). Benjamin Franklin: Quotes: quotable quote. *https://www.goodreads.com/quotes/103000-without-continual-growth-and-progress-such-words-as-improvement-achievement.*

2. Cohn, D'Vera & Taylor P. (2010, December 10). Baby boomers approach 65 – glumly. *Baby Boomers Approach 65 – Glumly | Pew Research Center.*

3. Cohn, D'Vera & Taylor P. (2010, December 10). Baby Boomers Approach 65 – Glumly. *Baby Boomers Approach 65 – Glumly | Pew Research Center.*

4. Massachusetts Body of Liberties (2021). Synopsis of the history of the Massachusetts body of liberties. *https://www.mass.gov/service-details/massachusetts-body-of-liberties.*

5. Bestor, A. (1964). The American civil war as a constitutional crisis. *The American Historical Review, 69*(2), 327-352. doi:10.2307/1844986.

6. Schwartz, B. (2015). The Emancipation Proclamation: Lincoln's many second thoughts. Soc 52, 590–603). https://doi.org/10.1007/s12115-015-9954-7.

7. The White House Briefing Room: (2021, July 10). A proclamation on Juneteenth day of observance June 18, 2021: Presidential actions. *A Proclamation on Juneteenth Day of Observance, 2021 | The White House.*

8. Peck, E. (1979). Wife beating in the nineteenth-century America, 4 Victimology: *An International Journal, 60*, 60-63.

9. Epstein, D. (1999). Effective intervention in domestic violence cases: Rethinking the roles of prosecutors, judges, and the court system: *Yale, J.L. & Feminism, 11*(1), 3. *https://digitalcommons.law.yale.edu/yjlf/vol11/iss1/3.*

10. Goldin, C. (1991). The role of World War II in the rise of women's employment. *The American Economic Review, 81*(4), 741-756. http://www.jstor.org/stable/2006640.

11. Dwyer, O. J. (2000). Interpreting the civil rights movement: Place, memory, and conflict. T*he Professional Geographer, 52*(4), 660-671, DOI: 10.1111/0033-0124.00255

Chapter Three

1. Noelle-Neumann, E. (1974). The spiral of silence a theory of public opinion. https://doi.org/10.1111/j.1460-2466.1974.tb00367.x.

2. Noelle-Neumann, E. (1974). The spiral of silence a theory of public opinion. https://doi.org/10.1111/j.1460-2466.1974.tb00367.x.

3. Crowe, J. (2016, November 9). 'Pollster Sabato on flawed predictions: 'Garbage in, garbage out.' *Pollster Sabato on Flawed Predictions: 'Garbage In, Garbage Out' | Newsmax.com.*

4. Williams, O., & Jenkins, E. (2019). A survey of black churches' responses to domestic violence. *Social Work & Christianity, 46*(4), 21-38. *https://doi.org/10.34043/swc.v46i4.110.*

5. Williams, O., & Jenkins, E. (2019). A survey of black churches' responses to domestic violence. *Social Work & Christianity, 46*(4), 21-38. *https://doi.org/10.34043/swc.v46i4.110.*

6. Grudem, W. (2010). Politics according to the Bible: A comprehensive resource for understanding modern political issues in light of scripture. *Politics According to the Bible: A Comprehensive Resource for Understanding Modern Political Issues in Light of Scripture: Wayne Grudem: 9780310330295 - Christianbook.com*

7. Williams, O., & Jenkins, E. (2019). A survey of black churches' responses to domestic violence. *Social Work & Christianity, 46*(4), 21-38. *https://doi.org/10.34043/swc.v46i4.110.*

Chapter Four

1. Murray, G. (1951). Reviews of book: The message if Fatima. *The Downside Review, 69*(215), 98–100. https://doi.org/10.1177/001258065106921511

Chapter Six

1. Goodreads (2021, July). Benjamin Franklin: Quotes: Quotable quote. *Quote by Winston Churchill: "The farther back you can look, the farther forw..." (goodreads.com)*

CPSIA information can be obtained
at www.ICGtesting.com
Printed in the USA
LVHW051132141021
700415LV00017B/257

9 781662 826757